LISTENING TO SURVIVORS

Listening to Survivors

FOUR DECADES OF HOLOCAUST MEMORIAL WEEK AT OREGON STATE UNIVERSITY

Edited by Katherine E. Hubler

Oregon State University Press   Corvallis

Cataloging in publication data is available from the Library of Congress.

ISBN 978-1-962645-24-9 paper; ISBN 978-1-962645-25-6 ebook

♾ This paper meets the requirements of ANSI/NISO Z39.48-1992
(Permanence of Paper).

First published in 2024 by Oregon State University Press
Printed in the United States of America

Oregon State University
OSU Press

Oregon State University Press
121 The Valley Library
Corvallis OR 97331-4501
541-737-3166 • fax 541-737-3170
www.osupress.oregonstate.edu

*Oregon State University Press in Corvallis, Oregon, is located within the traditional
homelands of the Mary's River or Ampinefu Band of Kalapuya. Following the
Willamette Valley Treaty of 1855, Kalapuya people were forcibly removed
to reservations in Western Oregon. Today, living descendants of these people
are a part of the Confederated Tribes of Grand Ronde Community of Oregon*
(grandronde.org) *and the Confederated Tribes of the Siletz Indians* (ctsi.nsn.us).

Contents

* denotes speakers who also became Oregonians

Foreword
The Best of Us
PAUL KOPPERMAN

One by one, survivors of the Holocaust are passing on. Now is the time, therefore, when we should recognize the achievement of these men and women and should recognize their importance to humanity.

Fortunately, in a sense the survivors can continue to speak for many years to come. Much of their testimony has been video-recorded and is available digitally through the United States Holocaust Memorial Museum, the USC Shoah Foundation, and on sharing platforms like YouTube. Thousands of survivors have published accounts of their experiences during the Holocaust, and of what they witnessed. Thousands, too, have left behind letters and diaries detailing the world of the Shoah, including those who, like Anne Frank, did not survive it. So, the stories can continue to be told. We can only hope that humanity will continue to hear and to heed.

It was not, for that matter, always the case that there was widespread interest in the survivors or in the Holocaust itself. For more than three decades after the liberation of the camps and collapse of Nazi Germany brought an end to the war against the Jews, this genocide was not high in the public consciousness of Europe or the United States. The reasons for such indifference were complex, but perhaps at the core was a sense that although the Holocaust was horrific, it was just another example of "man's inhumanity to man," and little advantage to society would be gained by learning or teaching the subject.

During the 1980s, this attitude changed. Although earlier the Holocaust was seldom taught at university, now an ever-increasing number of courses devoted to the subject were introduced. At the same time, progressively more schoolteachers began to introduce it to their classes. In the decades since, these tendencies have only increased. And the survivors have played a major part in this.

At Oregon State University, in Corvallis, we have observed Holocaust Memorial Week since 1987—a full week, often spreading into a second one, of events that recall and teach about the Shoah, but also about other campaigns of genocide, large-scale violations of human rights, and the issue of group-on-group hatred. Those who have spoken during OSU Holocaust Memorial Week have included many prominent scholars, who have drawn large audiences and have educated them on vital issues. But the largest audiences—almost always standing-room-only—have turned out for the survivors. And while all speakers are applauded, only survivors receive standing ovations, often a series of them.[1]

Despite the ovations, there are strong disincentives for survivors to share their stories with the public. Those who speak or write of their wartime experiences, and particularly the camp survivors among them, are by the nature of their task required to return to a circumstance of terror, a circumstance that saw them lose parents and siblings, a circumstance that left them shattered. So why do many survivors choose to share such memories? No, not for the money; in fact, most of them decline to take honoraria. Not for notoriety. Rather, what moves them is the opportunity to have a positive influence on their audience.

Although they appear in a number of venues, many survivors who speak publicly of their wartime experiences prefer to do so before young audiences. One of these is Joe Alexander, an Auschwitz survivor, who explains the preference this way: "They say that 70 percent of the children I talk to never heard of the Holocaust, so that is why it is important to speak to them to let them know what happened. To prevent another Holocaust, I am doing as much as I can."[2]

Another messenger with a purpose was Miriam Kominkowska Greenstein, who after the war settled in Portland, Oregon, and then devoted the last three decades of her life to speaking in thousands of schools throughout the Pacific Northwest—including, thankfully, Corvallis. When she spoke, she regularly allotted some of her time to sharing happy memories of her childhood in Poland, before switching to the Holocaust years, notably her time in Auschwitz. But she would also devote part of her talk to the general issue of group-on-group hatred and the huge role of antisemitism in bringing about the Final Solution and making it so murderous. She would conclude by saying emphatically, "The answer to the Holocaust is . . . DON'T HATE!"

Survivors have served the cause of Holocaust remembrance not only by speaking and writing, but also by helping to found institutions that teach. Henry Friedman, who spoke in Corvallis during HMW 2018, endowed and helped to establish a Holocaust center in Seattle. A number of survivors, notably Eva Aigner, were instrumental in establishing a Holocaust memorial in Washington Park in Portland, where visitors could learn and reflect.

Likewise, survivors are important advocates for Holocaust education—on all levels, but most prominently at the K-12 level. Alter Wiener, who endured five camps during the war, moved to Portland late in life and immediately offered himself to the schools as a speaker, not only on the Holocaust but on other human-rights cataclysms like the assault on Darfur. In 2018, working with a remarkable teenage girl, Claire Sarnowski, who had developed a sense of mission after she heard him speak, Al initiated a campaign to promote Holocaust education throughout Oregon. Sadly, he did not live to see this effort through, but in 2019 the state legislature passed, overwhelmingly, a bill to mandate teaching the Holocaust and other genocides in Oregon public schools. The state legislators who chiefly sponsored this bill, Rob Wagner, Janeen Sollman, James Manning, and Dallas Heard, dedicated it to Al's memory.

Few if any historical episodes can match the power of the Holocaust to encourage people to consider the ultimate question of history, "Why?" Without the survivors to remind us, this genocide might have joined the many crimes against humanity that are remembered only slightly and are accounted for by such clichés as "man's inhumanity to man," which implies no lesson or remedy.

Notes

1   Many recordings from past Holocaust Memorial Week events can be accessed at https://holocaust.oregonstate.edu/videos.
2   Joe Alexander addressed audiences at Oregon State University in May 2023.

Preface

Survivor accounts are vital to Holocaust and genocide education. Although no single individual experience could encapsulate the Holocaust in its entirety, the personal story of a single survivor can serve as an entry point for attempting to understand the overwhelming, collective human tragedy perpetrated by the Nazis and their collaborators during World War II.[1] While maps and statistics offer a comprehensive overview of sites of persecution and mortality figures, first-person testimony can humanize these statistics and flesh out the experiences of suffering, resistance, and loss at the scale of an individual or family. These testimonies also demonstrate the personalities and resilience of the survivors and those they lost, reflecting the humanity and richness of spirit of individuals who deserve to be recognized as more than simply "victims" or statistics.

This volume presents the voices of nineteen survivors, as well as two witnesses, who shared their personal experiences with audiences at Oregon State University and the broader community as part of Oregon State University's Holocaust Memorial Week observance, which launched in April 1987. Prompted into action by antisemitic activity within the Corvallis community, faculty worked closely with the Oregon Holocaust Resource Center (now part of the Oregon Jewish Museum and Center for Holocaust Education), local community members, city and religious leadership, and public educators to create an educational and commemorative program.[*] The program hosted its first survivor speaker, Fred Manela of Eugene, Oregon, in 1989. Since then, nearly thirty survivors and witnesses have shared their testimony and reflections during

---

[*] See the Afterword for more information about the OSU Holocaust Memorial program's origins.

the annual weeklong observance that includes academic talks, student conferences, documentary screenings, and artistic performances. Many of these events and talks—including all of the Holocaust survivor testimonies featured in this volume—were recorded and are available to view at holocaust.oregonstate.edu/videos.

Each survivor account shared at OSU over the past four decades is unique. The survivors featured here experienced the Holocaust in Germany, Austria, Czechoslovakia, the Netherlands, Poland, Hungary, and Romania, often navigating within and across national borders to seek refuge from persecution. Their speeches recount revolts in Nazi-run killing centers, intimate friendships with Anne Frank and her family, medical experimentation conducted by infamous Nazi doctor Josef Mengele, and countless acts of defiance. Many of the speakers passed through the Auschwitz camp system, often deceiving the Nazis about their young age to prolong their lives by engaging in grueling work in concentration and labor camps. Some hid—in the homes and barns of helpers—to elude the Nazis. Some fled from the Nazis, with varying distances and degrees of success. Some received aid from neighbors and non-Jewish community members, while others experienced betrayal. Many settled in Israel and United States after the war. In fact, nine of the survivors featured in this volume called Oregon home.[2] The diversity of the testimonies and life stories of these survivors underscore that the Holocaust was a complex, transnational event during which one's experiences and chances of survival were contingent on geographic location, geopolitical circumstances, linguistic skills, economic resources, age, gender, and, often, pure luck.

When joined together, these survivor accounts also shed considerable light on the experiences of Jewish teenagers and children during the Holocaust. All the survivor testimonies in this work come from individuals who experienced the Holocaust as children under the age of eighteen. Jacques Bergman, the oldest survivor (born in 1923) featured in this work, was only fifteen years old when his parents sent him alone to Amsterdam in early 1939 as part of a "Kindertransport" to escape Nazi-occupied Austria. The youngest survivor in this book, Eva Aigner (born in 1937), was two when the war began and eight when Russian soldiers liberated the Budapest ghetto in which she, her mother, and her sister had been confined. While the Holocaust survivor experience is fundamentally atypical (the majority of European Jews perished in the Holocaust), the survival of Jewish children was particularly anomalous. While 33 percent of Europe's adult Jewish population survived the war, less than 11 percent of Jewish children lived to see the war end.

Readers of this work should bear in mind that survivor accounts are not "enclosed capsules of memory," but rather "constantly mediated, contested, and fragile acts of remembering."[3] Compelled to render into words the indescribable, survivors of atrocity actively "recount" their memories while subconsciously and simultaneously negotiating what is "tellable" and what they consider "hearable" by their particular audience.[4] This dynamic process of translation and adaptation is also at work when survivors pen memoirs for publication or provide formal testimonies to archival repositories. For that reason, survivor accounts of the Holocaust are rarely fixed and static. Subsequently, the memories and reflections imparted to the audiences at Oregon State University arose amid the particular dynamic with the audience in attendance, or—when speakers delivered prepared remarks—were shaped by expectations about the potential audience. In addition to excerpts from survivors' accounts, this volume also includes speakers' responses to impromptu audience questions. Since the act of transcription itself shapes survivor accounts and their reception by the audience of readers, the textual excerpts of the speeches featured in this volume deliberately include the speakers' pauses, sighs, and stops and starts of speech to indicate intrusions of memories or emotions that words cannot easily convey.

Purpose of Book

The experience of the Holocaust is central to this volume, but its content invites a broader analysis of the dynamics of bigotry, persecution, and genocide, as well as the role of individual agency in perpetuating or resisting oppressive structures. As their testimonies and educational outreach work attest, the survivor speakers featured in the following pages were profoundly aware that government-led persecution tends to cascade; an assault on the rights and lives of one marginalized group is often accompanied by further assaults against other vulnerable populations. The survivors witnessed this historical lesson firsthand, as the genocidal actions the Nazis perpetrated against European Jews frequently intertwined with the persecution and murder of non-Jewish targets of the Nazi regime during World War II. The book's key themes and organization are informed by this intersectional awareness and by the Anti-Defamation League's "pyramid of hate," a curricular tool that conceptualizes genocide as a culmination of prejudiced and antidemocratic ideas, behaviors, and actions that deprive a vulnerable group of its rights and safety, leading to physical violence and mass murder.

The following chapters present Holocaust survivor testimony within a framework that will invite comparative analysis of the various stages of persecution that have historically preceded mass atrocities. They should also spark discussions about prejudice, racism, and discrimination in our current world and strategies for counteracting such forces and promoting human dignity. The essential questions and discussion questions that appear at the end of this work (see pages 157–163) correspond with each chapter's themes and provide educators and interested readers with a starting point for engaging in vital conversations. This book is written for anyone interested in the history of the Holocaust, its relevance to other genocides and atrocities, and for those curious about the plight of children and teenagers during the Holocaust.

This work was originally conceived of as a way to honor survivor-educators and support Holocaust and genocide education within Oregon. Several of the individuals featured in this volume—particularly Eva Aigner, Leslie "Les" Aigner, Miriam Kominkowska Greenstein, Chella Velt Meekcoms Kryszek, and Alter Wiener—served at the forefront of Holocaust commemoration in Oregon and public outreach to the state's young people since the mid-1990s, working in close coordination with the OJMCHE (and its predecessor, the Oregon Holocaust Resource Center).[5] This book aims to bring the history of the Holocaust to Oregon students and Oregon residents, highlight the important contributions from local survivors, and serve as a reminder of the state's connection to the Holocaust and commitment to genocide education and prevention. The book's chapters consequently align with Oregon's Holocaust and Genocide Education learning concepts[6] and the work contends with antisemitic and racist incidents in the state's recent past (see Chapter 5) as observed by local survivors.

Chapter 1 centers on experiences of discrimination and persecution before the onset of World War II and the organized mass murder of

Chella Velt Meekcoms Kryszek (*far left*), Jake Kryszek (*left of middle*), Miriam Kominkowska Greenstein (*right of middle*), and Judith Meller (*far right*), members of the Oregon Holocaust Memorial Committee, seated outdoors at the dedication of the Oregon Holocaust Memorial.

European Jews. It invites readers to reflect on the historical role that governments and official policies have played in normalizing prejudice and emboldening escalating acts of official and non-official persecution against vulnerable populations.[7] In addition, the chapter provides insight into the responses of non-Jewish community members during the initial phase of anti-Jewish discrimination and legal restrictions.

Chapter 2 explores the dilemmas and obstacles survivors and their families faced as they sought refuge from Nazi persecution and, after the start of war, increasing mortal danger.[8] Through a series of case studies, the chapter illuminates the uncertainties and staggering challenges that European Jews faced across geopolitical contexts, as well as the diverse and desperate forms that "refuge" took in an international political climate of isolationism and anti-refugee sentiment.

Chapter 3 puts into focus the myriad forms of resistance carried out by Jewish individuals—including children and teenagers—and communities during internment in Nazi-run ghettos, concentration camps, and killing centers.[9] The survivor recollections featured in the chapter encompass a range of nonviolent forms of resistance to preserve Jewish lives and traditions, as well as examples of violent uprisings against Nazi persecution.

Chapter 4 highlights individuals who overcame indifference and danger to oppose the Nazis' genocidal project and risked their lives to help—and save—the lives of others. This chapter features the personal recollections of two non-Jewish activists, George Wittenstein of the White Rose movement in Germany and Danish police officer and anti-Nazi saboteur Knud Dyby. It also includes survivor accounts of the acts of life-saving assistance they received during the war, sometimes from unlikely individuals.[10]

Chapter 5 recognizes and honors survivors' own contributions to transitional justice in the aftermath of the Holocaust. In this final chapter, survivors who are intensely engaged in educational, justice, and reconciliation efforts bestow advice to future generations and share their reflections on genocide prevention and forgiveness.[11]

Notes

1 Samuel Totten, "The Use of First-Person Accounts in Teaching about the Holocaust," *British Journal of Holocaust Education* 3, no. 2 (1994): 160–183.

2 Les and Eva Aigner, Ursula Bacon, Jacques Bergman, Miriam Kominkowska Greenstein, Chella Velt Meekcoms Kryszek, Laureen Nussbaum, Walter Plywaski, and Alter Wiener all resided in Oregon at one point.

3 Noah Shenker, *Reframing Holocaust Testimony* (Bloomington: Indiana University Press, 2015), 1.

4 Henry Greenspan, *On Listening to Holocaust Survivors: Recounting and Life History*, 2nd ed. (Saint Paul, MN: Paragon House), 2010.

5 As core members of the Oregon Holocaust Memorial Coalition, Les Aigner, Eva Aigner, Miriam Kominkowska Greenstein, and Chella Velt Meekcoms Kryszek, worked tirelessly toward the creation of the Oregon Holocaust Memorial in Portland's Washington Park, dedicated in 2004 to honor survivors of Nazi persecution who resided in Oregon and Southwest Washington, as well as their loved ones who perished during the war. In addition, the Aigners, and Miriam Kominkowska Greenstein, Chella Velt Meekcoms Kryszek, and Alter Wiener addressed thousands of the state's students in schools and libraries, many as part of the Speakers Bureau for the Oregon Holocaust Resource Center and, later, the OJMCHE. Although Alter Wiener did not move to Oregon until 2000, he became a leading voice in the call for mandating Holocaust in Genocide Education within Oregon public schools.

6 Holocaust and Other Genocides Learning Concepts (from OR SB664):

    (a) Prepare students to confront the immorality of the Holocaust, genocide, and other acts of mass violence and to reflect on the causes of related historical events

    (b) Develop students' respect for cultural diversity and help students gain insight into the importance of the protection of international human rights for all people

    (c) Promote students' understanding of how the Holocaust contributed to the need for the term "genocide" and led to international legislation that recognized genocide as a crime

    (d) Stimulate students' reflection on the roles and responsibilities of citizens in democratic societies to combat misinformation, indifference, and discrimination through tools of resistance such as protest, reform, and celebration

(e) Provide students with opportunities to contextualize and analyze patterns of human behavior by individuals and groups who belong in one or more categories, including perpetrator, collaborator, bystander, victim, and rescuer

(f) Enable students to understand the ramifications of prejudice, racism, and stereotyping

(g) Preserve the memories of survivors of genocide and provide opportunities for students to discuss and honor survivors' cultural legacies

(h) Provide students with a foundation for examining the history of discrimination in this state; and

(i) Explore the various mechanisms of transitional and restorative justice that help humanity move forward in the aftermath of genocide.

7 Chapter 1 supports Oregon Holocaust and Other Genocides SB664 Learning Concepts a, d, e, f, h.

8 Chapter 2 supports Oregon Holocaust and Other Genocides SB664 Learning Concepts b, d, e, f.

9 Chapter 3 supports Oregon Holocaust and Other Genocides SB664 Learning Concepts d, e, g.

10 Chapter 4 supports Oregon Holocaust and Other Genocides SB664 Learning Concepts d, e, f, g.

11 Chapter 5 supports Oregon Holocaust and Other Genocides SB664 Learning Concepts b, c, g, i.

Acknowledgments

I feel privileged to have had the opportunity to spend the past three years revisiting and reflecting on the moving stories and urgent messages delivered by survivors and witnesses of the Holocaust who have contributed to Holocaust Memorial Week at Oregon State University. I remain in awe of the courage, resilience, and energy of the speakers who have visited our community, and I have gained a renewed appreciation for the tireless educational and outreach efforts of the Oregon-based survivor community. I sincerely hope that the present work amplifies their mission and messages.

This book is four decades in the making. It reflects the time, energy, and goodwill of hundreds of Oregon State faculty, staff, and students, as well as local religious leaders, educators, and community members who have served on the Holocaust Memorial Committee since 1987. This hard work, bolstered by generous financial contributions from program donors, has helped make possible forty years of transformative educational and commemorative events. Thank you all for your efforts and continued support.

I relied on the assistance of many wonderful people to assemble and frame this volume. I leaned heavily on my colleagues and fellow Holocaust Memorial Committee members. Given his thirty-year service as chair of the committee, Paul Kopperman's institutional knowledge and guidance were invaluable as I compiled this work. In addition to penning the foreword and contributing to the afterword, Paul also provided essential feedback and additions to the introduction. Kara Ritzheimer helped shape the thematic structure of the book and provided key insights and editing notes for the initial sections of the book. This work is also indebted to the skills and assistance of Natalia Bueno and Robert Peckyno, who filmed many of the speeches featured, handled technical

aspects of HMW events, and oversaw the digitization of event recordings. I thank my students Rebecca Murray, Liam Hughes, and Dalton
Chambers for their careful transcription assistance. As they can attest,
auto-captioning applications are far from perfect, and many of our older
recordings of speeches needed to be captioned manually.

I am grateful for the assistance of the team at OSU Press, particularly Kim Hogeland, who helped in tracking down and securing rights to
some of the images used here. I also extend thanks to the outside review-
ers for their keen suggestions, which enriched the book and improved
its structure as an educational resource. I greatly appreciate the financial
support of the Oregon State University School of History, Philosophy,
and Religion.

Nicole von Germeten deserves special acknowledgment for making this volume a reality. During her tenure as director of the School
of History, Philosophy, and Religion, Nicole organized faculty support
for the work and shepherded the book proposal through its early stages
at OSU Press. I am grateful for her sharp insights, sage advice, and her
confidence in my ability to see the multifaceted project through to the
finish line.

Thanks to the Oregon Jewish Museum and Center for Holocaust
Education; Laureen Nussbaum; Holocaust Center for Humanity in
Seattle, Washington; Oregon State University Special Collections and
Archives Research Center; Archives of the YIVO Institute for Jewish
Research; United States Holocaust Memorial Museum; CANDLES
Holocaust Museum and Education Center; akg-images; Dr. Joachim
Castan, Filmkontor; and Sankar Raman for permission to reproduce the
images in this volume.

Introduction

While this edited collection focuses on the voices and experiences of survivors, an awareness of Nazi racial ideology, persecutory tactics, imperialist ambitions, and genocidal policies during World War II is essential to comprehending the realities Jewish Europeans faced during the Holocaust. This section provides key historical context to situate the testimony of the speakers featured in this volume. It also details the impact of Nazi racial policies on Jewish children and teenagers and could serve to help frame other Holocaust accounts or memoirs produced by individuals who experienced the Holocaust during their youth.

Jewish Life in Europe before World War II
Education about the Holocaust tends to deal more with Jewish death than with Jewish life. It is reasonable that scholars and students of history have devoted keen attention to the dynamics of genocide in order to better understand and try to prevent atrocities in the future. Nevertheless, it is vital to acknowledge Europe's vibrant Jewish communities, individuals, and cultures before they were targeted by the Nazis. Their lives—not only their deaths—matter. After all, the Nazis intended not only to murder Jewish people but also to erase the rich legacy of Jewish culture and Jewish traditions in Europe.

Jewish communities have been a part of European society for centuries. Settlements on the Mediterranean coast grew during the first and second centuries, after Judea was absorbed into the Roman Empire and the Jews, who had unsuccessfully rebelled against Roman rule, had been expelled. Jewish communities gradually emerged all over Europe. As Europe was increasingly Christianized in the Middle Ages, coexistence with Christian communities tended to be peaceful, yet Jews occasionally experienced large-scale, violent attacks—or "pogroms"—particularly during the Crusades (1095–1300s) and the Black Death (1347–1351).[1] For the most part, church leaders condemned these physical attacks on Jews due to the shared religious heritage of Christianity and Judaism. They also permitted Jews by and large to continue to carry on their traditions. Yet tolerance did not equal acceptance.

Church and secular leaders worked to limit Judaism's appeal and spread by imposing legal restrictions that thrust boundaries between Jewish and Christian communities and subordinated Jews to Christian authorities. In many regions, secular and religious leaders barred Jews from most professions and guilds, prohibited them from owning land and residing near Christians, and periodically expelled them from entire kingdoms.[2] Such expulsions brought a major shift in the distribution of European Jews, generally from the west to Poland and regions or states to the east or southeast of it. Often, however, the Jews were restricted in terms of where they could live. In regions of western Europe where Jews were still permitted, they were often forced to reside in walled neighborhoods of towns and cities, as allocated by local authorities.[3] In eastern Europe, most Jews lived in villages known as *shtetls*. The centuries-long legacy of economic restrictions—some of which persisted into the 1800s—led in some regions to a higher statistical representation of Jews within the limited professions from which they were not expressly excluded, such as trading, banking, law, and medicine.

Despite restrictions and periodic pogroms, Jewish communities in Europe demonstrated both resiliency and dynamism as they developed distinct regional cultures and branches of Judaism. The Sephardic tradition emerged in Spain, but after Jews were expelled from the Iberian peninsula during the 1490s, it was carried to regions of the comparatively tolerant Ottoman Empire, particularly the Balkans and southern Europe, as well as to the Netherlands. The Ashkenazic Jewish tradition was forged in central Europe, most notably in Germany, and would greatly influence Jews in central, eastern, and northern Europe.[4] Historically, both Sephardic and Ashkenazic groups had strong ties to Orthodox Judaism, marked by a rigorous adherence to traditional Jewish law and custom, religious rituals, and dress. Although forms of Orthodox Judaism would remain prevalent in many communities in Poland and Eastern Europe, over time different interpretations of religious texts and traditions led to the development of various branches of

Judaism with diverse expressions of piety and Jewish customs. During the nineteenth century, Reform Judaism, a movement that originated in Germany, arose to adapt and balance ancient traditions with aspects of modern life made possible during industrialization. Influenced by intellectual, political, and nationalist currents of the late-nineteenth and early-twentieth centuries, secular Jewish identities, movements, and communities also emerged, which pivoted away from a primary focus on Jewish religious traditions. Within the more liberal Jewish groups, assimilation was often more pronounced than it was among traditional Jews. Some adherents intermarried, and some accepted baptism. But a considerable majority continued to identify as Jews. Furthermore, the general community that would endure the Holocaust was predominantly Orthodox. Of the approximately 9.5 million Jews living in Europe as of 1933—the year when Hitler came to power in Germany—6.7 million (over 70 percent) resided in Poland and Eastern Europe, the centers of Orthodoxy.[5]

The gradual evolution of Judaism and Jewish communities in various European regions over two millennia means that there is no single, archetypal Jewish community, nor one monolithic experience of Judaism experienced by all European Jews in the decades before World War II and the Holocaust. The survivor speakers featured in this volume, who themselves hailed from eight different countries, attest to the diversity of European Jewish life and experiences. Some of these speakers were raised in Orthodox Jewish families and attended religiously oriented schools, while others came from less observant and even secular backgrounds and attended public school. Some grew up in small villages and led lives centered on traditional Jewish practice and principles. Others lived more cosmopolitan, secular lives in cities. Some had a Christian parent or grandparent(s). The families of some speakers were more assimilated; they identified strongly with the national culture of their region and often had relatives who had served in the armed forces. They saw themselves as being integrally linked to their respective nations and imagined that these nations saw them as such. In most cases, however, the speakers were familiar with Yiddish and Hebrew and could be described as bicultural, as well as bilingual or multilingual. Chapter 1 provides insights into some of the survivor speakers' family and cultural life before the world of their childhood was toppled by the Nazis.[6]

Nazi Germany and "Enemies of the Nation"

When Adolf Hitler was appointed chancellor of Germany on January 30, 1933, Germany was still a constitutional democracy, and most Germans did not support the National Socialist German Workers' [Nazi] Party. In fact, Hitler had lost the 1932 presidential election and even in the Nazis' most successful parliamentary election in July 1932, they attracted less than two-fifths of the vote. For Hitler and his inner circle, seizing total political control in Germany would require destroying the democratic system, eliminating political enemies, and preventing opposition from the German population. They set to work at these tasks with staggering speed and efficiency.

By September 1933, Hitler had succeeded in transforming Germany into a one-party dictatorship under his personal control. As his first step, Hitler launched a merciless assault on political opponents and the law-making process when, in late February, he blamed communists for a fire that destroyed the building where the German parliament (the Reichstag) met and ordered mass arrests of thousands of German Communist leaders, many of whom were tortured or shot. One month later, on March 22, 1933, the Nazis opened the first concentration camp[7] in Dachau for the imprisonment of political opponents. The very next day, Hitler convinced members of the Nazi-majority parliament to pass the "Enabling Law," which gave Chancellor Hitler authority to rule by decree. The Enabling Law fundamentally ended democracy in Germany by allowing Hitler alone to make laws, bypassing the approval of the democratically-elected parliament and president. Hitler completed the final step toward authoritarianism in September when he outlawed all political parties in Germany, with the exception of the Nazi party.

Hitler initially focused on intimidating, silencing, and imprisoning all political opponents of Nazism, most of whom were non-Jewish communists, socialists, and liberals. That the Nazis pursued noncompliant, non-Jewish Germans first for imprisonment in concentration camps set the general population—who had read about the camps in German newspapers—on edge.[8] The Nazis did not hide the creation of domestic concentration camps from the general population since the awareness of the punishments meted out at these camps served as a deterrent to dissent. In **Chapter 2, George Wittenstein**, a member of the White Rose resistance movement, highlights the dangers he and his non-Jewish

German friends faced—and the ultimate price many of them paid—while participating in an anti-Nazi resistance movement. Hitler's message to all Germans was clear: Fall in line or face swift punishment.

By July 1933, just four months after Dachau opened its gates, the Nazis had interned nearly 27,000 people in concentration camps. While camp conditions before WWII began were wretched and sometimes lethal, the Nazis intended that camp incarceration could serve a rehabilitative function for the initial population of inmates, who might decide to change their ways—particularly their problematic political, spiritual, or sexual ways—if they were ever released from the camp. The early camp population did include some Jewish people, although their arrests generally corresponded with their political beliefs—those arrested were often communists, socialists, and liberals, or they had publicly criticized the Nazi regime. (German Jews were not sent to concentration camps solely on the basis of their Jewishness until late 1938.) A number of Jehovah's Witnesses could also be found among the early camp prisoners. Although Jehovah's Witnesses made up a tiny fraction of the German population, Nazis considered them disloyal pacifists since their religious beliefs restricted them from taking oaths or serving in the national military.

The National Socialist regime also persecuted a variety of vulnerable minorities whom Hitler and Nazi racial ideology regarded as threats to Germany's biological strength. As early as the 1920s, in the pages of *Mein Kampf*, Hitler declared that Germany's national strength and security depended upon the biological strength of "racially-pure," non-Jewish Germans, whom he deemed members of a so-called "Aryan" race.[9] Hitler's deliberate use of the term "Aryan"—co-opted from the work of late-nineteenth and early-twentieth-century linguists and racial science theorists—instead of "German" or "Germanic" to describe the so-called "master race" also lent the façade of scientific authority to Nazi racial theory and policies.[10] As the following pages detail, Hitler and Nazi scientists and leaders emphasized the importance of "Aryan" racial health and purity to justify a range of persecutory policies that included economic and social segregation of Jews and forced sterilization and euthanasia of people with disabilities.

For their lack of contribution to reproducing "Aryan" Germans, the Nazis attacked gay communities. The regime outlawed organizations and institutes that pursued homosexual rights, they raided gay bars, and arrested men[11] suspected of homosexuality, many of whom faced castration. Roughly 10,000 gay German men were interned in domestic concentration camps; they frequently faced cruelty and ostracization from other inmates, and 6,000 perished.[12] Nazi leaders hoped to intimidate gay men into abandoning their "homosexual tendencies" through abuse, punishment, and sometimes sexual re-education.

Since the Nazis paired their concern for the growth of the "Aryan" German population with an obsession over the quality and purity of the "racial stock," they persecuted Afro-Germans, as well as the Sinti and Roma[13] people (sometimes referred to pejoratively as "Gypsies") living in Germany. Both groups were subjected to increased police harassment in the mid-1930s, and the Sinti and Roma would later face sterilization as "asocials" and deportation to concentration camps, and eventually mass murder, during the war. Although small in number within Germany, Germans of African descent experienced job loss, evictions, and even forced sterilization and imprisonment for "miscegenation." The Nuremberg Laws of 1935 were extended to the Sinti, Roma, and Afro-Germans, who faced restrictions on their citizenship rights, including a prohibition on marrying "Aryans."[14]

In the early months of his power, Hitler also moved against Germans with physical or mental conditions and disabilities. Even though many were classified as "Aryan," Nazi leaders and members of the Nazi medical community deemed them unfit for life and took steps to strip away their autonomy and, ultimately, their lives. As historian Doris Bergen explained, "Nazi planners measured the value of a human life by its contribution to the national community, not by some inherent worth."[15] A July 1933 law ordered the sterilization of individuals experiencing what the regime categorized as "hereditary diseases," including deafness, blindness, epilepsy, depression, chronic alcoholism, and certain physical deformities. The law also extended to people categorized by Nazi personnel as "feebleminded," an ambiguous term used to describe a broad range of mental conditions and cognitive disabilities. These laws tended to target populations who were already vulnerable and often frequently dehumanized by proponents of the eugenics movement. Many of those forcibly sterilized were already institutionalized and separated from their families and the general public.

Nazi Antisemitism and Anti-Jewish Legislation before WWII

The Nazis considered Jews to be the most threatening element in German society. In the eyes of the Nazis, political opponents and Jehovah's Witnesses posed security risks to Germany, while the Roma, Sinti, Germans of African descent, homosexual men, and people with disabilities endangered the racial health of the nation. But Jews were a double threat, both political *and* racial dangers to the nation.

While Nazi notions of race were constructed to serve ideological interests and provide a pseudo-scientific veneer to support Nazi policies, the Nazi conception of a "Jewish race" was particularly problematic. As the outgrowth of a monotheistic social group in the ancient Near East, Jewish identity itself is complex and even today does not often fit discretely within contemporary categories of religion, ethnicity, nationality, or race. "Judaism," Doris Bergen explains, "was and is a religion *and* a living community."[16] As such, Jewish religious beliefs (which extend across multiple branches of Judaism), Jewish ancestral heritage, and Jewish cultural practices are components of Jewish identity, each of which could serve as a basis for belonging in the Jewish community and for self-identification as Jewish.

Despite the complexities of Jewish identity, Nazi rhetoric insisted that Jews and "Aryans" were fundamental opposites, contrasting in both character and biology, given the supposed degeneracy of the former and the superiority of the latter. Nazi officials and "racial science" experts were flummoxed, however, when it proved impossible to distinguish Jews from "Aryans" based on physical characteristics or other "scientific" metrics. Debates about how to determine with precision if a person was "Jewish" raged among members of the Nazi Ministry of Interior's "Committee on Population and Race" in the mid-1930s.[17] Although the regime never budged in its insistence about the existence and danger of a biological "Jewish race," Nazi officials ultimately decided to lean heavily on religiosity to determine Jewish identity; the 1935 Nuremberg Laws, discussed in greater detail below, legally categorized as Jewish anyone with three or more grandparents who had practiced Judaism.

Jews served as a convenient scapegoat for Hitler and the Nazis. Since Jews had been subjected to prejudice, stereotyping, periodic social restrictions, and occasional waves of violence within Europe since the fourth century, Nazi propagandists had centuries of antisemitic tropes and stereotypes to mine, morph, and deploy in a modern, twentieth-century context. German Jews made up less than 1 percent (roughly 500,000 people) of the total German population, yet Nazi propaganda blamed them for Germany's loss of World War I, the economic disaster of the Great Depression, the rise of communism, and seemingly every problem that befell Germans. Nazi claims about Jews defied coherent logic: Jews were both arch-capitalists *and* arch-communists. Jews were lazy and never worked hard, yet somehow tirelessly controlled the levers of global power and worked high statesmen like puppets to maintain Jewish dominance. Furthermore, the cosmopolitan and corrupt "Jewish spirit" was blamed for all decadence and immorality, including homosexuality, promiscuity, alcoholism, and crime in Germany.

In April 1933, the Nazi government began a "legal" assault on Jews' civil liberties and economic livelihoods. The "Law for the Restoration of the Professional Civil Service" barred participation by anyone deemed "non-Aryan" in both high-ranking professions like judges, but also low-level jobs like street cleaners and postal workers. The law applied to people who had one "non-Aryan parent or grandparent." As a result of the April laws, Jewish doctors, lawyers, judges, and civil servants were prohibited from carrying out their jobs in the civil administration. Other legal proclamations limited the numbers of Jewish students that could attend schools and universities. A new set of laws, the aforementioned Nuremberg Laws, promulgated in September 1935, however, officially categorized Jews as biological and political outsiders. The "Law for Protection of German Blood and Honor" prohibited marriage and sexual relations between Jews and so-called "Aryan" Germans. It also made it illegal for Jews to fly the German flag. The second, "Reich Citizenship Law," stripped away most civil and political rights from Jews by defining them as mere "subjects," no longer citizens, of the German Empire.

The regime created these laws with the intent of removing Jews from positions of authority, socially isolating and impoverishing Jewish communities, and compelling Jewish Germans to emigrate. Even before WWII and deportations began, it was a challenge for most German Jewish families to keep themselves fed and in a warm place after 1933. Daily life was full of anxiety in a society orchestrated to remind Jews that their presence was not desired in Germany. Most non-Jewish Germans did not oppose the Nazis' restrictive anti-Jewish laws for two reasons. First, this persecution was typically orderly, generally nonviolent, and carried the façade of legality. Second, such policies tended to bring economic advantages for non-Jewish Germans who took over the jobs, businesses, and apartments vacated by Jews. This systematic isolation and removal of Jews from daily economic, social, and political life in Germany ultimately resulted in the "social death" of Jews in Germany years before the concerted efforts to physically destroy German Jewish communities began during World War II.[18] In such a difficult environment, some Jewish families elected to leave Germany. For instance, the year after the Nuremberg Laws were announced, **Laureen Nussbaum's family (see Chapters 1 and 4)** fled their native Frankfurt to seek refuge in Amsterdam. Indeed, the Nazis had hoped that their antisemitic legal maneuvers would encourage Jewish emigration out of Germany. Nevertheless, Germany was "home," and many Jews held out hope that they could persevere despite the restrictions on Jewish life that grew each year.

It wasn't until the pogroms of November 1938, which followed on the heels of the German invasion of Austria and the Sudetenland (the outer portions of western Czechoslovakia), that it became apparent that Germany was fundamentally unsafe for Jews. In the months leading up to the pogroms, the Nazis escalated their attacks on Jews in their expanding Reich. They rescinded all legal protections for synagogues, sent to concentration camps Jewish "anti-social" men and those who did not have German citizenship, and, in October, deported 17,000 Polish Jews to the border of Poland, where they were abandoned with no official aid and were restricted from entering Poland. Among those Polish Jews expelled to the Polish border was **Lucille Eichengreen's father, Benjamin Landau (see Chapter 1)**, who had lived in Germany since the end of World War I. The assassination of a German diplomat by a Jewish student in Paris (whose Polish family had been expelled from Germany) served as sufficient pretext to initiate a widescale attack on Jewish lives, property, businesses, and religious centers across Germany and Austria. The Nazis called the orchestrated pogroms of November 9–10 *Kristallnacht* ("Crystal Night" or "The Night of Broken Glass") due to the tremendous amount of property destruction visited upon Jewish homes, businesses, and synagogues, although an increasing number of recent scholars opt to use the term "November Pogrom" when describing this event to avoid using the Nazis' terminology and to emphasize more accurately the event's violent nature.

These attacks represented the first time the Nazi government publicly condoned violence against Jews. Crowds invaded Jewish orphanages and hospitals, vandalized homes and businesses, and burned synagogues. Police officers and firefighters refused assistance to Jewish community members. Perpetrators of the attack, led by members of the *Sturmabteilung* (Stormtroopers, or SA) and the Hitler Youth, killed at least 100 Jews during the pogroms, and many others died in the aftermath as a result of brutal assaults. In addition, around 30,000 Jewish men were systematically apprehended and sent to German concentration camps. Although **Marion Blumenthal Lazan (Chapter 1)** was only four years old at the time, she recalls the chaos of the night, which culminated in her father's arrest and internment in Buchenwald. This marked the first time that Jews had been sent to concentration camps solely because they were Jewish, and not due to political beliefs, citizenship status, or criminal records.

While Jews frequently pondered leaving Germany in the mid-1930s, the escalation of persecution in 1938 had convinced many who had been previously reluctant to emigrate that a life outside of Germany was the only solid option. Immigration visas were difficult to come by since potential countries of refuge, such as the United States, did not look favorably upon Jewish immigration and severely restricted the number of Jewish refugees they would take in. Nazi policies forced Jews to surrender the majority of their assets before leaving Germany, which made Jewish refugees particularly unattractive to foreign governments who were already concerned that immigrants would become social and economic burdens. In addition, populations still experiencing the Depression and limited employment feared economic competition from immigrants and fed resistance to raising immigration quotas. **Ursula Bacon (Chapter 2) and Marion Blumenthal Lazan (Chapter 1)** describe the difficulties their families faced when trying to find a country willing to allow them entry. In total, about 60 percent of the Jewish population (between 270,000 and 300,000 Jews) did leave Nazi Germany. Unfortunately, around 30,0000 who left Germany for other parts of continental Europe later found themselves again under Nazi control during WWII.

The Kindertransport

As attacks on Jewish communities intensified in late 1938, private citizens and Jewish aid organizations launched a special rescue effort, known as the *Kindertransport* (Children's Transport), to bring to safety Jewish children from within Nazi-controlled regions. Following the November 1938 pogrom, the British government announced it would expand and expedite the visa process to allow into its borders an undetermined number of unaccompanied children under the age of seventeen. Volunteers and aid societies organized the transport of children, primarily via train, to ports in the Netherlands or Belgium, at which point children would travel via passenger ships to Harwich, England. From there, children would go to foster homes or orphanages in England; private individuals and aid societies subsidized their care. Priority was typically given to orphans or children whose parents were unable to care for them, either due to economic hardship or incarceration in concentration camps. The first transport arrived in Great Britain in early December 1938 and included children whose Jewish orphanage in Berlin had been destroyed the prior month. The program was established with the understanding that it would be temporary and that children would reunite with their parents when it was safe to do so. Unfortunately, most of the parents of the rescued children perished during the Holocaust. In total, around 10,000 children were saved as a result of the effort.

Most of the Kindertransport children disembarked in England, but around 1,800 remained in the Netherlands. Although this branch of the Kindertransport is often overlooked, a number of the speakers at OSU's Holocaust Memorial Week were personally affected by this rescue effort. **Jacques Bergman's (Chapter 2)** parents sent him on a transport out of Vienna, Austria, when he was fifteen years old. Unable to get on a transport all the way to England, Bergman ended up in Holland in December 1938. Beginning in January 1939, the Dutch government arranged to house children under fourteen with foster families, some of whom were also Jewish, but fifteen-year-old Bergman was moved into a group home and worked in several factories before he was apprehended by the Nazis in 1942. The family of **Marion Blumenthal Lazan (Chapter 1)** had migrated to the Netherlands in January 1939. They took on the responsibility of looking after 125 refugee children upon their arrival. **Chella Velt Meekcoms Kryszek (Chapter 2)**, a Jewish native of the

Netherlands, spent part of her childhood in a Jewish orphanage in The Hague. Chella later recalled the moment that fifty sobbing German children—displaced by the November pogroms—suddenly appeared in the orphanage. Although she was only ten years old at the time, Chella spent the dark hours trying to comfort an inconsolable five-year-old German girl who cried out for her mother.

The legacy of the Kindertransport is complex. The refuge provided for children was a humanitarian gesture funded and sustained by the goodwill of private organizations and individuals, but it was also a minimal and politically calculated action by governments that generally sought to restrict immigration from refugees of Nazi Germany and limit state funding for refugees.[19] Children—but not their endangered parents—were granted entry into England, as the children, who were not viewed as economic competitors, were more likely to elicit sympathy and voluntary aid. Still, many other countries would not even go so far as to issue emergency visas for endangered children. In the United States, the Wagner-Rogers Bill, which would have allowed for the temporary admission of 20,000 child refugees (under the age of fourteen) from Nazi Germany, was too unpopular to even go up for a vote in the House or Senate. A national Gallup poll conducted in January 1939 revealed that only 26 percent of US respondents agreed with a proposal to "permit 10,000 refugee children from Germany to be brought into this country and taken care of in American homes"; 67 percent of American respondents opposed the plan.[20]

World War II and Genocide

The Nazi invasion of Poland in September 1939 marked the end of the Kindertransport and the beginning of six years of Nazi military aggression in Europe. We cannot fully understand the Holocaust without considering the nature and course of World War II. At the most basic level, the murder of six million European Jews would have been impossible without an expansionist war that brought Europe's Jewish population—most of whom resided east of Germany—into the Nazis' reach as German forces marched toward the USSR. With each territorial gain in the east, more Jews came under Nazi control. The war itself also helped facilitate genocide, logistically and ideologically. As historian Doris Bergen observed, "War provided killers with both a cover and an excuse for murder; in wartime, killing was normalized, and extreme measures could be justified with arguments about the need to defend the homeland and defeat the enemy."[21]

In pursuit of Hitler's goal to colonize large swaths of Central and Eastern Europe and exploit the resources and people on those lands, German forces committed numerous atrocities and crimes against humanity, as they terrorized local communities, displaced millions of civilians, and subjected many to forced labor and abuses, including murder. The brutal methods by which the Germans waged war, particularly against civilians, were informed by Hitler's racial ideology and goal of acquiring *Lebensraum*, or "living space," for Germans. Hitler claimed that a nation or "race" must continue to expand and conquer others, or else face extinction. Therefore, the creation of a new German Empire and access to vast natural resources—in part to replace what had been stripped from Germany after its loss in World War I—was essential to Hitler's vision for the restoration of Germany and the "German race." Nazi racial ideology justified the subjection, enslavement, and even murder of so-called "inferior" peoples east of Germany—Poles, Russians, Ukrainians, Belorussians, Lithuanians, other Slavic peoples, and European Jews—so that the German race could flourish. Hitler's writings about "race and space" echoed the same kinds of concepts that had been commonly used to justify the colonization and subjugation of Indigenous communities within Africa, coastal regions in Asia, and large swaths of North and South America in the nineteenth century.

Since the Germans encountered so many Jews in their initial eastward advancement, the 1939 invasion of Poland marked the beginnings of the next Nazi phase of Jewish persecution—the large-scale "ghettoization" of Jews from regions that Hitler sought to resettle with ethnic Germans. It's not clear at first what Nazi policymakers had planned for the residents of Polish ghettos, but they certainly did not intend for Jews to be part of the new German empire. Official documents suggest that the Nazis considered plans for shipping off European Jews to Madagascar, establishing a permanent Jewish "reservation" in Lublin, Poland, or simply working ghettoized Jews to death. The first ghettos were intended initially as temporary holding places for Jews before they could be sent to the Lublin district, the site of the proposed reservation. But once the plan for a Jewish reservation was abandoned by Nazi officials in the spring of

1940, Nazi officials began to "seal off" these concentrated populations of Jews in urban areas like Łódź and Warsaw. The labor of ghettoized Jews would be exploited by local industries. Instead of paying Jewish laborers, industrialists would pay the German government, who would use a meager portion of funds to purchase food and medical supplies for the ghetto population. As more German troops flooded into occupied Poland in the spring of 1941, Jews faced additional expulsions from their home communities, which led to substantial overcrowding in ghettos. Over half a million Polish Jews died in ghettos and labor camps. Most of these deaths were the result of disease, starvation, and brutality. Even in larger ghettos that included hospitals, nursing homes, and orphanages, conditions were poor, and food and medicine were in short supply.

As World War II progressed and German forces encountered larger Jewish populations—particularly after the invasion of the USSR in 1941—calls for a "final solution" to the "Jewish Question" intensified. The pursuit of a "war of annihilation" in the Soviet Union gave way to a new policy regarding the treatment of Jews in territories invaded by German forces. Whereas previously SS killing squads targeted Jewish males of military age and those suspected of participating in partisan resistance movements, by the summer of 1941 they began murdering all Jewish persons—men, women, children, and the elderly.

The SS sent special mobile killing squadrons, called *Einsatzgruppen*, into Soviet regions to carry out the murder of Jewish civilians after the German military had subdued the region. Nazi agents relied on the cooperation of local populations to identify Jews in their communities and recruited additional triggermen from war-torn populations in the Baltic states and Ukraine. In exchange for their horrific service as executioners, SS officials offered local men an array of enticements including release from deadly POW camps, promises of postwar independence from Soviet rule, and the possibility of obtaining food, alcohol, and Jewish property. In total, the *Einsatzgruppen* and their numerous auxiliaries murdered between 1.5 and 2 million Jews on the Eastern Front, at killing sites that were often within walking distance from the victims' homes, schools, and workplaces. This wave of murder is commonly referred to as the "Holocaust by bullets," which was rather different from the more distant and industrialized manner of mass murder made possible in killing centers. The largest incident of mass murder carried out by the *Einsatzgruppen* and their assistants took place in Babi Yar, a ravine outside of Kiev, where over 33,000 Jews—mostly women, children, and elderly individuals—were killed in only two days over the course of September 29 and 30 in 1941.

The historical record suggests that by late 1941, Hitler and Nazi leaders had officially resolved to murder all European Jews—11 million in total. In January 1942, Reinhard Heydrich, a high-ranking official in the SS, convened the Wannsee Conference. This was an assemblage of high-ranking civilian and Nazi officials, and the meeting's purpose was to both share information and facilitate this plan. Although the "Holocaust by bullets" was currently underway in Soviet territory, Nazi officials were wary of utilizing the same tactics to "remove" Jews from Western and Central Europe since mass shootings near villages and cities were disruptive and ran the risk of exposure to the Western Allies. Nazi officials resolved, then, to construct killing centers east of Germany. Instead of killers traveling to the victims, the victims would be transported, often by rail, to killing sites that would utilize more indirect and mechanized methods of mass execution, such as asphyxiation by carbon monoxide and poison gas. Chelmno was the first killing center used by Nazi forces in December 1941. In 1942, four new killing centers at Belzec, Sobibor, Treblinka, and Auschwitz-Birkenau became operational, just a few months following the Wannsee Conference. In total, the Nazis murdered nearly three million European Jews within killing centers.

Children and the Holocaust

Age did not shield children from the brutal consequences of Nazi racial policies. In fact, children with disabilities in Germany, primarily from "Aryan" families, were the very first group that Nazis targeted for systematic murder. Just before instigating WWII, Hitler personally authorized officials to begin secretly "euthanizing" babies and young children, and required hospitals to report births of children who exhibited physical deformities, mental disabilities, or paralysis. At least 10,000 German children with disabilities were murdered in special "pediatric clinics" by medical personnel using overdoses of medication or starvation.[22] Viewed through the lens of competitive biological politics, all "unhealthy Aryan" and "racially inferior" babies and children represented existential threats to "healthy Aryan" Germans, even if their young age meant that they did not pose an immediate danger.

The Nazis murdered nearly 90 percent of Europe's Jewish children during the war.[23] Of the six million Jews killed by the Nazis during World War II, nearly 25 percent—roughly 1.5 million—were under the age of eighteen. By murdering Jewish children, the Nazis believed they were leading a campaign to destroy a population of "future enemies" whose destructive capacities would grow over time. While some members of the *Einsatzgruppen* had recoiled at the idea of shooting Jewish children in mass executions that followed the German army's advance into Soviet zones in summer 1941, SS leader Heinrich Himmler reminded his men that Jewish children must be killed because of their dangerous potential in the future: if allowed to live, they could grow up to seek vengeance for the deaths of their parents and their people.

The strategic cruelty deployed in the genocidal campaign to destroy the Jewish communities, families, and children is deeply troubling. Beginning in the summer of 1941, Nazi agents shot Jewish children in Soviet regions *en masse* alongside their mothers and grandparents. (Their fathers were either shot first or shipped to a camp for forced labor.) Horrifically, the *Einsatzgruppen* often did not waste bullets on babies or small children, and instead allowed them to fall into mass graves where they would slowly suffocate beneath other bodies and soil. During "Aktions," or Nazi roundups of Jews in ghettos and occupied villages, babies were often shot on sight while in their cribs or carriages. Older children—those who could walk—were typically among the first deportees from ghettos to concentration camps and killing centers, as they were deemed incapable of forced labor to benefit the German economy.[24]

The experiences of **Jack Terry (Chapter 4)** and **Stephen Nasser (Chapter 3)** and other persons who lived to see liberation from a Nazi camp at war's end were exceptional, a fact they readily admit. The vast majority of children who entered camps and killing centers were selected for immediate execution. When space permitted, Nazi officials admitted only able-bodied people between the ages of fifteen and fifty for work within a camp. In rare cases where children were admitted into camps as prison laborers, they were not spared the grueling work, wretched living conditions, exposure to the elements, gnawing hunger, and brutality from guards that characterized life in the camps. Babies who arrived at the camps were typically sent directly to gas chambers, accompanied by an older sibling, grandmother, or mother.[25] A small number of children, especially twins, were admitted to camps for the purpose of Nazi medical experimentation, as **Eva Mozes Kor (Chapters 3 and 5)** recounts.

Family separation and loss was a ubiquitous feature of the Jewish experience of the Holocaust; most Jewish families, especially those in Eastern occupation zones, had been dismantled before children disembarked at a Nazi camp. Although the dynamic varied during different moments in the war, fathers typically faced the first removals from the family unit, as Nazi forces apprehended and dispatched them to camps for the purposes of labor, but also to render their household more vulnerable to deportations (earlier in the war) or immediate mass execution (during the "Holocaust by bullets"). As a result of the initial removal of men, the population of ghettos tended to be dominated by women, along with children and the elderly. Deportation "Aktions" in the ghetto further aimed to remove "nonproductive" children from any remaining parents and the elderly from their work-age adult children.

Children had to grow up fast and adapt to new family dynamics and the loss of parents or contend with the limits of their parents' ability to protect them. For instance, **Jack Terry (Chapter 1)** witnessed his father, his protector, emotionally crumble at the dinner table and start to "fade away" shortly after the Nazis invaded his town and began to ghettoize it. Holocaust scholar and child survivor Nechama Tec recalled that her parents often reminded her that "childhood was a luxury that Jewish children could not afford."[26] Tec's parents took time to carefully explain to their daughter about the developing dangers for Jews in Poland and did their best to prepare her for life in the ghetto and, later, in hiding. Other parents, when confronted with unthinkable new realities, sometimes kept their children in the dark about initial dangers and worst-case scenarios, which was something that **Ruth Kluger (Chapter 3)** especially resented. Regardless of the strategies that adults pursued to protect the Jewish children in their lives, the children eventually confronted the brutal realities of Nazi rule and occupation. Although Ruth Kluger's survival was ultimately owed to her resourceful if tempestuous mother, Ruth spent much of her Holocaust girlhood second-guessing her mother's decisions and inability to protect her children during Nazi persecution. **Chella Velt Meekcoms Kryszek (Chapter 2)**, whose doting father was killed at Auschwitz, lamented her father's heart-breaking predicament when the entire family was apprehended from their hiding spot. Kryszek explained, "Later in years when I had children myself, I thought [about] the suffering of the parents, before they went to their death, that they couldn't help their children."

The oral testimony of child survivors, as well as surviving—if fragmented—evidence about and produced by children during the war, testify to the resiliency, adaptability, and defiant spirit of children during the Holocaust in the face of a series of increasingly deadly situations. Since Nazi policies and curfews restricted Jewish employment and mobility within cities, Jewish children often took on additional responsibilities to provide for their family. Against strict Nazi policy, eleven-year-old **Miriam Kominkowska Greenstein (Chapter 2)**, whose looks enabled her to "pass" among non-Jewish Poles, shed her star and went out in public to buy necessary food to supplement the meager rations they were provided after the Nazis invaded her hometown in Poland. To make up for the absence of parents or grandparents, children in ghettos often took care of younger siblings, worked, bartered, smuggled, snuck into restricted areas, and even stole in order to keep their families afloat and feed themselves.[27] **Walter Plywaski (Chapter 1)** entered the Łódź ghetto at age ten and was able to avoid deportation through his aunt's connection to controversial ghetto leader Chaim Rumkowski, as well as his work in the electrical department.[28] In an effort to avoid being selected for execution and prolong their life in a Nazi-run work camp, many older children lied about their age, succeeding at times. Both **Ruth Kluger (Chapter 3)** and **Jack Terry (Chapter 1)** owed their survival in work camps to deceiving others about their ages. Each of these acts of adaptation and deception with the intention of saving their own lives—and those of their friends and family—were acts of resistance to the Nazis' genocidal project.

Children survived by their wits and luck, but they also found ways to try to cope with the ever-present misery, cold, hunger, and death in the ghettos and camps. Ghetto children frequently played games, some of which mimicked their plight as a way of processing their new realities.[29] According to Nicholas Stargardt, "Children sought to express the difficulties and tensions and, by the very act of dramatizing them, to overcome them."[30] In **Chapter 3, Marion Blumenthal Lazan** describes the games with which she filled her days as a ten-year-old at Bergen-Belsen. The pebble search game that she regularly played probably served as a welcome distraction from her surroundings, but it was also a manifestation of her understandable fixation on her family's survival. Some children became engrossed in learning, when schooling or books were available. **Ursula Bacon (Chapter 3)** relished the short-lived underground school that operated in the Shanghai ghetto. While education was illegal in the camps, Ruth Kluger lost herself in the underground classes arranged for children in Theresienstadt and then, in more dire circumstances within Auschwitz, in the pages of a smuggled textbook. When possible, children also wrote about their experiences. With a lot of ingenuity and canny bartering, **Stephen Nasser (Chapter 3)** constructed a makeshift diary and acquired a rare pencil. The act of personal reflection and documentation of the experience of Nazi persecution was both a way of processing the impossible and an expression of resistance.

Occasionally, children benefited from the pity, sympathy, and aid from older camp prisoners. Arguably the most famous and successful example of child aid within the camps was the child rescue program at Buchenwald, run by the well-organized and well-established "underground" of prisoners, many of them Jewish communist inmates. The underground created a special *Kinderblock* (children's block), units of child inmates who received exemption from hard labor assignments, benefited from extra food rations donated by fellow prisoners, and, as much as it was possible, were not selected for deportation to other camps. Children from all backgrounds were admitted into the *Kinderblock*, including Jewish children, and, as a result, a total of 904 children's lives were spared.[31] **Ruth Kluger (Chapter 3)** and **Jack Terry (Chapter 4)** also benefited from the sympathy and aid from fellow camp inmates. A young female prisoner—a stranger to Kluger—who was tasked with assisting a doctor making "selections" voluntarily vouched that twelve-year-old Ruth was fifteen and stronger than she appeared. Jack Terry survived his first brush with death when he snuck away from a mass execution of boys during the Nazi liquidation of the Bełżyce ghetto and disappeared into a nearby line of "able-bodied" men destined for a work camp, who made room for him in the line. Thirteen-year-old Jack stood on stones so that he appeared taller and fit in with the men around him. During his time at Flossenbürg, Jack, the youngest prisoner in the camp, was shielded from grueling manual labor tasks and a "death march" by non-Jewish inmates Milos Kucera and Carl Schrade.

Within Nazi-occupied regions, most Jewish children who survived the Holocaust did so in hiding. Most families split up in order to hide children, and they did so for practical reasons. Children tended to garner more sympathy from non-Jews, and they consumed less food than adults, an important consideration during the war and Nazi occupation. Jewish children who could "pass" as "Aryan" were sometimes integrated into Christian families and given new identities, allowing them to hide in plain sight by pretending to be non-Jewish. Although a new Christian identity afforded Jewish children mobility and contact with the outside world, children in these circumstances were under intense pressure to bury their past and vigilantly maintain their cover stories and conceal any mannerisms or information that could raise suspicion and jeopardize their lives and those of their Christian helpers. Jewish children were also hidden clandestinely—out of the public eye—by sympathetic individuals, families, and religious—typically Catholic—institutions. Regardless of the manner in which they were concealed, hidden children lived in constant danger of being discovered as Jews and were vulnerable to wartime deprivations and sometimes even abuse from their keepers. Due to their impressionable ages and the dire necessity of rapid adaptation to their new circumstances, hidden children—like their counterparts in the Kindertransport—often clung to aspects of their new identity and new religion and occasionally lost track of who they had been before being separated from their parents. The postwar period was an especially difficult period of transition for both hidden children and those who had been part of the Kindertransport program, who frequently found themselves orphaned. In interviews with survivors who had lived in hiding as children in the Netherlands, sociologist Diane Wolf noticed the recurring refrain expressed by many of them: "*My war* began after the war."[32]

In rarer circumstances, hidden children maintained ties with family members while evading Nazi detection and capture. This was the case after all for Anne Frank, the most famous hidden child of the Holocaust. Although **Chella Velt Meekcoms Kryszek's** family **(Chapter 2)** did not have a designated family hiding place like the Franks did, her father was able to keep tabs on his daughters during their eighteen-month concealment by various members of the Dutch Underground. Chella, sometimes

accompanied by her older sister, was permitted a limited range of movement indoors while sheltering with a series of different Underground
host families before her capture and deportation to Westerbork and,
ultimately, Auschwitz. **Henry Friedman's (Chapter 2)** time in hiding in
rural Poland was shared with his pregnant mother, younger brother,
and teacher in an attic space so small that even young Henry could not
stand up. Friedman's period in hiding was intensely claustrophobic and
restrictive, marked by extreme hunger and the haunting experience of
"choosing," at the age of fourteen, what should be done with his newborn
sister, whose cries would have certainly betrayed the family's location to
officials and led to the deaths of all of the Friedmans and their Christian
rescuers. Children, even those in hiding, were not spared the "choiceless
choices" that pervaded the Jewish experience of the Holocaust.

Liberation

Although survivors welcomed the end of the war, liberation was bitter-
sweet, tempered by tremendous trauma and loss. Most surviving Jewish
children were orphans by the end of the war. This was the case for **Jack
Terry, Thomas "Toivi" Blatt, Miriam Kominkowska Greenstein, Lucille
Eichengreen, Alter Wiener, and Stephen Nasser.** Some children, such
as **Eva Mozes Kor, Chella Velt Meekcoms Kryszek, and Walter Plywaski**
managed to survive Nazi internment with a sibling, but lost generations
of family members. While the appearance and assistance of Allied soldiers was celebrated and appreciated, many of the speakers who visited
Oregon State continued their fight for their survival. The majority of them
spent weeks and months in hospitals recovering from typhus, malnutrition, and various infections. These were vulnerable weeks for Holocaust
survivors in general, and a tragic number of them never recovered from
late war illnesses, extreme malnutrition, and the toll of grueling death
marches from camps in the east. In fact, 20,000 to 30,000 of the 90,000
Jews liberated from Nazi camps died within the first few weeks after the
war's end.[33] As Les Aigner described in his speech at Oregon State, the
Allies tried their best to nurse camp survivors back to health, but many
died from lack of access to necessary medication, as well as their inability
to digest the rich food they initially received.

  After their bodies recovered, survivors went in search of family and
a safe place to restart their lives. While some of the speakers featured in

this volume emigrated to Israel after 1948 (such as Toivi Blatt and Eva Mozes Kor), the majority came to the United States within a few years after the war's end. Nine of the speakers would eventually call Oregon home, some of them drawn by family members who had settled in the state just before the start of World War II. Due in large part to the efforts of the Oregon Émigré Committee, which worked in conjunction with national and local Jewish organizations, as well as Portland-area families, one hundred Jewish refugees from Germany and Austria had settled in the Portland area by Christmas 1938.[34] In 1947, the Oregon Émigré Committee reported that Portland "had assimilated" a total of 400 "refugees of Nazi persecution" before the war began.[35] Jacques Bergman's older brother, Leo, was among this group, as was Miriam Kominkowska Greenstein's uncle.

Survivor Contributions to Justice and Education

In the immediate aftermath of destruction—of their families, communities, and former lives—many Holocaust survivors began to document and speak about their experiences. Understandably, not all were emotionally willing or even physically capable of recounting the trauma and losses they endured during the war. But those who came forward did so with purpose; they sought to promote justice and provide an accurate and public record of the Nazi genocidal project in order to counteract Nazi denial and obfuscation. To be clear, many Jewish targets of Nazi persecution had pursued such goals during the war itself, risking their lives to assemble reports and photographs to be smuggled through underground networks to the Allies when possible, or to be buried away until they could be unearthed after the war. Upon liberation, however, centers for Jewish documentation of the war—led by surviving Jewish historians and religious scholars—flourished across Europe, feverishly collecting and preserving survivor testimony to be used as evidence in Nazi war crimes trials.[36] Individual survivors provided eyewitness testimony in countless postwar trials, most visibly in the 1961 televised trial of SS Lieutenant Colonel Adolf Eichmann. In vital ways, Holocaust survivors contributed to an emerging postwar international legal system based on the protection of human rights and human dignity. The survivors featured in this volume continue this survivor-led legacy of promoting justice and human rights through their educational outreach.

It behooves us, as readers in the twenty-first century, to listen to survivors' messages in the pages that follow. Survivors have gone to great lengths and have revisited unimaginable pain in order to recount their experiences to us. As bearers of history, survivors impart important lessons for our present and our future. While survivors cannot tell us exactly *how* to prevent discrimination, genocide, and warfare, their accounts reveal the dynamics by which persecution and mass murder arise. Their experiences demonstrate how rapidly legal discrimination against one group can escalate and widen to other vulnerable populations. They remind us how fragile democracy and constitutional rights can be and urge us to remain vigilant and take action when individuals, institutions, and governments seek to dehumanize and discriminate against targeted groups. In sharing their stories, survivors also honor those who were lost and bear witness for those who cannot speak for themselves. The testimonies that follow offer a precious glimpse of the loved ones and Jewish communities that perished.

Notes

1 The term "pogrom" originated in late-nineteenth-century Russia to describe the violent attacks and massacres perpetrated against Jews in Eastern Europe at that time. The word means "riot" or "destruction" in Russian. In its contemporary usage, a "pogrom" is an organized attack on the lives and property of a marginalized group in order to eliminate the group, or terrorize the group into leaving a particular area.

2 These expulsions typically occurred in the wake of Christian attacks on Jews during times of religious zeal and warfare (such as the Crusades) or during economic downturns. Jews were banned from England in 1290 and France in 1306. In 1492, following the success of the "Reconquista" to push out Muslim forces, Ferdinand and Isabella expelled Jews from Spain.

3 This type of a residential area became known as a "ghetto," the word coming from the name of a section in Venice where Jews were settled in 1516.

4 Both Sephardic and Ashkenazic Jews used Hebrew script, but Sephardic Jews spoke Ladino (an outgrowth of Spanish) whereas Ashkenazic Jews spoke Yiddish (a language related to medieval German).

5 Statistic from the USHMM via the American Jewish Yearbook. https://encyclopedia. ushmm.org/content/en/article/ jewish-population-of-europe-in-1933-population-data-by-country.

6 Most of the survivors of the Holocaust who addressed audiences at Oregon State University did not speak extensively about pre-WWII Jewish culture, a tendency that can be attributed to their relatively young ages during the late 1930s and 1940s, as well as the time constraints of their 60- to 90-minute speaking engagements. Fortunately, many of the survivors featured in this volume have elaborated on their communal life and religious practices in published memoirs and recorded oral testimonies housed at repositories such as the United States Holocaust Memorial

Museum, the USC Shoah Foundation, and the Oregon Jewish Museum and Center for Holocaust Education.

7 The very first concentration camps had been created by European colonizers in Africa in the late 1800s to detain local civilian populations that Europeans deemed "disruptive" or potentially dangerous during times of rebellion against the colonizers. The Nazi *Sturmabteilung* (Stormtroopers, or SA) was originally tasked with resurrecting these camps within Germany and overseeing the brutal treatment of prisoners, who were often condemned to hard labor, poor living conditions, and constant abuse from guards and even fellow prisoners. People interned within German concentration camps were not subject to traditional due process—they often had no trial or access to a legal defense and could be detained indefinitely—and authorities were not required to produce evidence that the individual had committed an official crime.

8 Within two years of Dachau's existence, most Germans were familiar with the popular rhyme, "Dear God, make me dumb [mute], That I may not to Dachau come." "Lieber Herr Gott, mach mich stumm / Das ich nicht nach Dachau komm." Morris Janowitz, "German Reactions to Nazi Atrocities," *American Journal of Sociology* 52, no. 1 (1946): 141.

9 A word about "race": As we understand today, race is a social construct, a concept first developed by Western European thinkers beginning in the Enlightenment era to classify and hierarchically rank groups of humans according to perceived physical and intellectual features. The modern field of genetics has debunked the idea that people assigned to a particular race actually share the same biological makeup. Studies conducted since the Human Genome Project have determined that as much genetic diversity can be detected *within* the same so-called racial group as between different racial groups. Although race is not real in a *biological* sense, the *social* influences and impacts of race, racial categories, and ideas about racial hierarchy are indeed very real and have had a significant impact on notions of identity and lived experiences of groups. As the case study of the Nazi era illustrates, throughout history, self-proclaimed dominant "racial" groups have deployed concepts of race to justify the segregation, "legal" subordination, economic exploitation, and even murder of groups they regard as "racially inferior." In the present day, scholars and public policymakers continue to pay attention to racial categories and demographic data broken down by "race" to understand the legacies of racial categorizations and their continued impacts on communities.

10 The linguist Friedrich Max Müller first used the term "Aryan" in the 1850s to describe Indo-European language groups. Müller noted their distinction from Semitic languages, spoken by Jews. Subsequent racial theories suggested that "Aryans" were light-skinned people from ancient India who migrated to Europe and became the forebears of European culture. Doris Bergen, *War and Genocide: A Concise History of the Holocaust* (New York: Roman & Littlefield, 2016), 52–53.

11 Lesbian women were sometimes harassed, arrested, and punished as "asocials," but the regime did not systematically persecute or try to "re-educate" them. Claudia Schoppmann, *Days of Masquerade: Life Stories of Lesbians During the Third Reich*, trans. Allison Brown (New York: Columbia University Press, 1996); Samuel Clowes Huneke, "The Duplicity of Tolerance: Lesbian Experiences in Nazi Berlin," *Journal of Contemporary History* 54, no. 1 (January 2019): 30–59.

12 Peter Hayes, *Why? Explaining the Holocaust* (New York: Norton, 2017), 207.

13 According to the USHMM, "Roma are a European ethnic group whose ancestry can be traced to modern-day India and Pakistan. Many Romani groups refer to themselves by different names, such as Sinti, Kalderashi, or Lalleri. Sinti are Roma with historical roots in German-speaking lands. In many languages, Roma are often referred to by exonyms (names or labels assigned to a group or place by outsiders).

In English, this word is 'Gypsy,' which is generally considered derogatory." "Glossary,"
USHMM Holocaust Encyclopedia, https://encyclopedia.ushmm.org/en/glossary.

14 For more about the Nuremberg Laws, see pages 8 and 9.

15 Bergen, *War and Genocide*, 159.

16 Emphasis added. Bergen, *War and Genocide*, 18.

17 Claudia Koonz, *The Nazi Conscience* (Cambridge, MA: Harvard University Press, 2003), chap. 7.

18 Marion A. Kaplan, *Between Dignity and Despair: Jewish Life in Nazi Germany* (New York: Oxford University Press, 1998).

19 Jennifer Craig-Norton, *The Kindertransport: Contesting Memory* (Bloomington: Indiana University Press, 2019).

20 "The Immigration of Refugee Children to the United States," USHMM Holocaust Encyclopedia. https://encyclopedia.ushmm.org/content/en/article/the-immigration-of-refugee-children-to-the-united-states.

21 Bergen, *War and Genocide*, vii.

22 Within a matter of months, the children's "euthanasia" program would eventually expand into the "T4 program," a larger program to murder adults with disabilities in Germany.

23 The situation was grimmest in Poland, where only around 5,000 Jewish children (less than 1 percent of the prewar population of 1 million) lived to see the end of the war. For overall comparison's sake, 33 percent of Europe's adult Jewish population survived the war.

24 At the Wannsee Conference, Nazi officials had agreed that Jewish labor could be exploited as a way of benefiting the German economy and war effort, while also hastening the death of Jewish forced laborers.

25 Even if the mother was deemed able-bodied enough to work, many Nazi agents decided—after facing violent resistance from mothers—that it was often too much trouble to force a mother to part with her baby or young child and more "humane" to allow them to stay united and face execution together. In addition, many mothers and grandmothers elected to accompany their condemned young ones to the gas chambers in order to spend a few moments more with them and comfort them.

26 Nechama Tec, Introduction to *Children during the Holocaust*, by Patricia Heberer (Blue Ridge Summit: AltaMira Press, 2011), 20.

27 Nicholas Stargardt, "Children," in *The Oxford Handbook of Holocaust Studies*, ed. Peter Hayes and John K. Roth (New York: Oxford University Press, 2010), 218–232.

28 Mordechai Chaim Rumkowski (1877–1914) led the Jewish Council in the Łódź ghetto and is known for his role in the deportation of thousands of Jewish children to the Chelmno killing center. Following the invasion of Poland, Nazi leaders ordered the creation of Jewish Councils in each community in order to disseminate and implement German orders, including orders to gather ghetto inhabitants for deportations to concentration camps and killing centers. By requiring high-ranking Jewish community members themselves to announce German orders and demand compliance from fellow Jews, the Jewish Councils became lightning rods for resentment, which led to discord in the Jewish communities. In September 1942, Rumkowski, after pleading with Nazi leaders to reduce the number of Jews for deportation, carried out Nazi orders to collect 20,000 people in Łódź —mostly children, the elderly, and those suffering from sicknesses—for deportation to Chelmno. The "roundup" process was grueling and heartbreaking—6,000 children were ripped away from their families and 500 people were shot attempting to flee. Admittedly, Nazi demands placed Rumkowski in an impossible position. Survivors of the Łódź ghetto, notably Lucille Eichengreen, have described Rumkowski as abusive and power-hungry. Gordon J. Horwitz, "An Overwhelming Presence:

Reflections on Mordechai Chaim Rumkowski and His Place in Our Understanding of the Łódź Ghetto," in *Jewish Histories of the Holocaust: New Transnational Approaches*, ed. Norman J.W. Goda (New York: Berghahn Books, 2014), 55-72; Lucille Eichengreen, *Rumkowski and the Orphans of Lodz*, with Rebecca Camhi Fromer (San Francisco: Mercury House, 2000).

29 Popular ghetto games included "Going through the gate," in which children took on the roles of Gestapo officers and forced laborers. The former searched the latter for contraband. The games of children in the Theresienstadt camp dramatized roll calls and the camp hierarchy. They even played a game called "Gas Chamber," in which they threw stones into a trench and mimicked human cries. Heberer, *Children during the Holocaust*, chap. 8.

30 Stargardt, "Children," 222.

31 The youngest child, Stefan Jerzy Zweig, was three and a half at liberation. Nechama Tec, Introduction to *Children during the Holocaust*, by Heberer, 30.

32 Diane L. Wolf, *Beyond Anne Frank: Hidden Children and Postwar Families in Holland* (Berkeley: University of California Press, 2007), 7.

33 Dan Stone, *The Liberation of the Camps: The End of the Holocaust and Its Aftermath* (New Haven, CT: Yale University Press, 2015), 19.

34 Statistic from Max S. Hirsch of the Oregon Émigré Committee. Shotwell Calvert, "Refugees in City," *Oregonian* (Portland, Oregon), December 25, 1938, 60.

35 "500 Refugees Due on Coast," *Oregonian* (Portland, Oregon), March 6, 1947, 10.

36 The Central Committee of Polish Jews furnished the Allied prosecutors at Nuremberg valuable evidence. Prominent institutions emerged in France (the Centre de Documentation Juive Contemporaine), Poland (Central Committee of Polish Jews, which included two surviving members of the Oyneg Shabes), Displaced Persons camps (Central Historical Commission), as well as Italy, Hungary, Sweden, and London. David Cesarani, "Challenging the 'Myth of Silence': Postwar Responses to the Destruction of European Jewry," in *After the Holocaust: Challenging the Myth of Silence*, ed. David Cesarani and Eric J. Sundquist (New York: Routledge, 2012), 15–38.

1
Reflections on Discrimination, Racism, and Stereotyping

> *This is the way mass murder starts. Not with a pistol shot, but by a titter and a smirk.*
> —Walter Plywaski (2004)

The survivors featured in this chapter experienced profound discrimination and social isolation well before the Nazis carried out the mass murder of European Jews during World War II. While the survivor speeches excerpted in Chapter 1 illustrate the devastating impacts of official antisemitic policies that restricted and policed Jewish livelihoods and families beginning in the mid-1930s, they also reveal the damage and danger wrought by "ordinary" community members whose apathy, antisemitic jokes, exploitative behavior, and cruelty were not always explicitly directed by government. These personal stories of survivors reveal a dangerous dynamic by which the introduction of Nazi-influenced "official" policies and propaganda—both of which depicted Jews as dangerous subhumans who needed to be isolated in order to protect the non-Jewish community—gave weight and validity to preexisting anti-Jewish tropes and prejudices, signaling to the broader public that Jews were neither fully human nor worthy of humane treatment. In such an environment, acts of prejudice and violence against Jews became normalized and tended to multiply and escalate in severity over time. Yet even in the face of increasingly difficult circumstances that included job losses, relocations, and physical attacks, the survivors whose speeches we read in this chapter highlight the tremendous resilience and perseverance demonstrated by Jewish families and, especially, Jewish children. We will further explore these twin themes of resilience and resistance in Chapter 3.

LAUREEN NUSSBAUM (B. 1927)

For many years, the life of Laureen Nussbaum (born Hannelore Klein) paralleled that of her childhood friend, Anne Frank. Like Anne, Laureen was born in Frankfurt, Germany, and her family fled to Amsterdam in 1936—three years after the Franks—to avoid Nazi rule. The Klein and Frank families socialized while in the Netherlands, and Laureen developed a friendship with Anne's older sister, Margot. Refuge in Holland was short-lived, as the Nazis invaded in May 1940 and began to implement anti-Jewish restrictions there. The two families' paths would soon diverge in 1942, when the Franks went into hiding to avoid deportation and the Kleins—due to the assistance from an unlikely source (see Chapter 4)—obtained life-saving documentation that classified them as a "mixed race" (part-"Aryan" and part-Jewish) family.

At the war's end, Laureen and her future husband, Rudi Nussbaum, forged a strong friendship with Anne's father, Otto Frank, the only surviving member of the Frank family. During her speech at Oregon State in 2014, Laureen explained, "We had sort of adopted him a little bit as an extra father in the family." In fact, Otto Frank was the best man at Laureen and Rudi's wedding. In 1957, Laureen and Rudi left the Netherlands to bring their family to the United States, settling in Portland, Oregon, just two years later. Laureen acquired a PhD at the University of Washington and taught in the Department of Foreign Languages and Literature at Portland State University

Laureen and Rudi Nussbaum's wedding in 1947, pictured with sisters and Otto Frank (father of Anne Frank) at the left, in the window frame. Courtesy of the Holocaust Center for Humanity in Seattle, Washington.

*until her retirement in 1989. In the following excerpt, Laureen describes
how the Nazi invasion of the Netherlands and the implementation of
anti-Jewish laws there affected her daily life.*

[F]irst in Germany, in my experience, we were marginalized. We couldn't
go to public school anymore. We had to go to Jewish schools. We couldn't
go to the theater; we couldn't go to the beach . . . not to the parks, not to
the forest. We were totally cut out of anything that was recreational or
cultural. So life became very, very narrowly focused. [Laureen and her
family eventually moved to Amsterdam in 1936 to escape oppression
from the Nazis within their native Germany.]

In the fall of 1941 [following the Nazi invasion of the Netherlands],
we were again sent to Jewish schools [in Amsterdam]. We couldn't go to
public schools anymore. In contrast to my [earlier] experience in Germany where a girl with whom I had walked to school every day in first
and second grade wouldn't walk with me in third grade anymore because
I had to go to Jewish school—which was in the same building, by the
way. . . . I never had any of those experiences in Holland. So that was
certainly positive about Amsterdam.

[W]e were totally excluded from anything cultural. We tried to . . .
keep our minds and brains alive by doing cultural things on our own.
There was chamber music; there was play-reading; there were poetry
groups. And I had brought from Frankfurt a Jewish play from the Jewish school that we did when I was a third grader. So I thought, "Well,
why shouldn't we entertain our parents and siblings by doing that play?"
Which was kind of risky because we had switched to Dutch so very, very
fast that for instance, for Anne [Frank], German was almost a foreign
language by then. For my younger sister also, German was a foreign language. My older sister and I were old enough . . . to still speak German
quite well. So, we put on that play in my parents' apartment. My parents
were always very generous . . . anything that needed to be done or celebrated could always be done at our house. We had a wonderful heavy
red velvet curtain between the dining room and living room, which just
looked like a stage curtain. So the dining room was the stage, and the
living room was the auditorium. And we put on this play called "The
Princess with the Nose." Although I am not entirely sure, I'm 90 percent
sure that Anne was the princess. She definitely was in the play. And I

definitely was the stage director. [T]hat's when I got to see [Anne] several times in the two weeks or so that led up to the performance. She was a fast study, and we had a great time doing the play.... We did it twice during the Christmas/Hannukah season of 1941. Everybody was very happy that we had gone to the trouble, and it was a great success. So that's when I saw Anne quite frequently. Otherwise, I didn't see much of her. She was younger and she and my younger sister did not go to religious education. My older sister, Susi, Anne, Margot [Frank], and I bicycled together. So I got to know Margot much better. And if I have any regrets about the international acclaim of Anne's diary, it is that maybe not enough justice is done to Margot, who was a wonderful girl, very scholarly, very ladylike, which I admired, because I was a tomboy. And [Margot was] just a very fine person really.

I mentioned that we could not partake of any cultural or recreational events anymore. What I did not mention was that, as of May of 1942, we had to wear the yellow star.

Laureen Nussbaum's ninth grade class in the Jewish School, Amsterdam in 1942. Laureen is in the second row, at the very center. Courtesy of Laureen Nussbaum.

This is my ninth grade class [in the Jewish School, Amsterdam] (*see photo on opposite page*). You can see the star on most of the people. A star is on the lady in front, the history teacher, the bookkeeping teacher next to her, the French teacher, who became a professor later on. He was a very fine teacher; he survived. But of the kids—the sixteen of us—four survived. The rest of them were killed in concentration camps. And so were at least two, if not three, of the teachers. I'm not entirely sure.

When I was in ninth grade, Anne was in seventh grade, her first year of high school in Holland. I don't have a picture of her with the star, but she had to wear the star just like everybody else . . . . everybody Jewish obviously. And then on July the 5th of 1942 . . . that's when someone came [to deliver an official message] that Margot had to report for labor service in Germany within ten days. The Franks took this as a signal [that their lives were in danger], and they went into hiding [the] next day. And [you know] what happened in hiding, of course, if you read [Anne Frank's] diary. Anne at first didn't know that the call was for Margot. She thought it was for her father. . . . But after a few hours, she found out what the true story was. And so the Franks went into hiding. . . .

When we came back to school in the fall of 1942 [after summer break], my then tenth grade class dwindled every day. . . . We started out as fifteen. I don't exactly know the number anymore. The next day we [were] thirteen. The next day we were nine. And we never asked whether so-and-so was in hiding or was deported. You just didn't ask questions. One of the reasons being that you didn't want to know what you didn't *have* to know, because you could always be apprehended and tortured and you could "spill the beans." So, it was just an unwritten law that you did not ask any questions about anybody that you were not the first person to help. If it was your responsibility to take care of a person, then of course you knew [whether they were in hiding or were deported]. But otherwise you didn't know. That was the rule of the game. . . .

But you have to picture the situation in the Jewish school as the classes dwindled. Every day, less children. I remember the chemistry teacher . . . once came to me desperate and said to me, "Your sister isn't doing any homework anymore." . . .

I said, "No wonder."

She was the only student left in her class. Can you imagine in 11th grade being the only student? Nobody else. Everybody else was either deported, or in hiding. So, of course the teachers were trembling in their boots, because they knew the moment all the children were gone, then their deferment would be annulled, and they would go [to a concentration camp]. So it's very hard to do your lessons, to do your algebra, to do your French irregular verbs—do all the things that you're supposed to be doing in school—knowing it's going to fall apart tomorrow. Those were very, very tough times.

MARION BLUMENTHAL LAZAN (b. 1934)

The Nazis were already in control of the German government when Marion Blumenthal Lazan was born, in a small town near Hannover (Hoya an der Weser) in 1934. Marion's family endured the onslaught of restrictive laws enacted against German Jews, which she chronicled during her speech delivered to the Oregon State University audience remotely via videoconferencing in 2020. Although Marion's parents initiated the administrative steps to move the family to the United States, the immigration process was slow and expensive. Following the violence of the November pogroms and the arrest of Marion's father, the desperate Blumenthals headed to the Netherlands in January 1939 where they were interned in the Dutch-run refugee camp, Westerbork, awaiting US immigration approval. Tragically, the Nazis invaded Holland the following year, took control of Westerbork, and deported the family to Bergen-Belsen in January 1944. In spite of all, Marion and her family survived the Nazi-run camps and immigrated to the US in 1948, finally using the steamship tickets they had purchased ten years earlier.

Life in the early 1930s in Germany was very much for my family as it is here for most of you today. Never did we think that the antisemitic incidents there would ever lead to very much. My father was in a successful shoe business in our small town. My parents, two-year older brother, and I lived comfortably, with my grandparents, above the shoe store. Life for Jews was made increasingly more difficult. And in 1935, the Nuremberg laws were formulated and enforced. . . . Jews were not allowed into theaters, into parks, or into swimming pools. All public schools were closed to Jewish children. Then there was the evening curfew for the Jews. Jews were only allowed to shop during specific hours of the day. And non-Jews were not allowed to shop in Jewish-owned stores. Non-Jews were just not allowed to associate with Jewish people. And then a big letter "J" for "Jew" was stamped on ID cards and on passports. These restrictions went on and on.

And it was then that my parents decided to make arrangements to leave the country. My grandparents, who were in their late seventies and ill, refused to leave their home and could not understand the urgency or the necessity of doing so. My grandparents passed away in 1938, just eleven days within each other. And soon thereafter, we received our necessary papers for our immigration to America. I was just four years old at that time. November 9, 1938, *Kristallnacht* or "Crystal Night." It was the "Night of broken glass" when the Nazis and their many followers smashed the windows and the storefronts of Jewish-owned stores, Jewish establishments, synagogues, and Jewish books were burned and destroyed. This was the beginning of a massive pogrom against the Jews in Germany, a massive verbal and physical assault against all German Jews. In reality, this was the beginning of the Holocaust. On November 12th, following *Kristallnacht*, the German government actually fined the Jewish population for the damage caused that night.[1] These imposed taxes were used to re-arm Germany. The night of *Kristallnacht* our apartment was ransacked. All valuables were thrown into a pillowcase and taken away. But worst of all was that they transported my father to concentration camp Buchenwald in Germany. All sorts of terrible stories were related to my mother, and we did not know if we would ever see my father again. He was released after three weeks only because our papers were in order for our immigration to America. And to think that just a few years prior, he had been awarded the Iron Cross for his military service in the German army of World War I.

We were forced to sell both our home and our business for a fraction of its worth. And soon thereafter, in January of 1939, we left for Holland, from where we were to sail to the United States. And for almost nine months while awaiting our quota number from the American State Department, my parents were assigned to take care of some 125 children. These young children had been sent by their parents from various parts of Europe to escape from the Nazis.[2] In December of that year, 1939, we were deported to the detention camp of Westerbork in Holland to await our departure date to America. Camp Westerbork was constructed by the Dutch to accommodate Jews from various parts of Europe.

In May of 1940, just one month before our planned departure date [to the United States], the Germans invaded Holland and we were trapped. All of our belongings, which were about to be loaded aboard ship, were burned and destroyed as the harbor of Rotterdam was bombed. Under Dutch control, Camp Westerbork was tolerable. My mother, father, brother, and I shared two small rooms. We all ate in a communal dining room, and at that time there was enough food for us, so that we did not go hungry. Adults were assigned to various work duties. My father worked to repair shoes. My mother worked in the kitchen. We children had a makeshift education and lived a very dull, stagnant life. Several months later, when the Nazi SS took over the command of Westerbork, we became acquainted with the ever-present, terrifying, 12-foot-high barbed wire. And there thousands of Jews were rounded up, many taken from their hiding places, as was Anne Frank and her family. Camp Westerbork became overcrowded. And it was at that time that we had to share our small quarters with another family. And then, the dreadful transports to the concentration and extermination camps in Eastern Europe began. This started in early 1942.

LUCILLE EICHENGREEN (1925–2020)

Lucille Eichengreen's (born Celia Landau) parents were natives of Poland but moved to Germany following the end of World War I to escape antisemitism and start a new life, eventually settling in Hamburg and opening a business. In the following excerpt from her 2017 speech at Oregon State University, Lucille describes her family's experiences as Polish Jews living in Nazi Germany at the onset of World War II, which culminated in their deportation to the Łódź ghetto in Poland in 1941. Following her liberation from Bergen-Belsen, Lucille delivered to British forces the names and addresses of SS guards, so they could be brought to justice. In the face of death threats for her actions, Lucille was resettled in France briefly before immigrating to the United States in 1946 and raising a family. Her 1994 memoir, From Ashes to Life: My Memories of the Holocaust, *recounts her journey in full.*

As a young, curious child I frequently overheard [my parents] talking in Polish and kept asking why they had left Poland. Their answers were short and too complicated for me to comprehend: "We are Jewish and life in Poland was often frightening. The Catholic Poles did not like us." As a preschooler, I accepted their words, not really knowing what they meant, but I realized that they obviously did not want me to learn Polish.

I started school in 1930, a semi-private, semi-Orthodox Jewish school for girls. My questions—"Why not a school in our neighborhood? Or in our area?"—always received the same answer. "You will be happier, and you will learn a great deal more in this school." My life at home was happy, carefree. And I knew I was loved by caring parents. And later by a little sister.

My life took a turn early in 1933. The incidents were very significant from the very beginning and way beyond the comprehension of a third grader in 1933. We overheard many remarks made by our parents, teachers, and hostile neighbors. We were often admonished by our parents and teacher not to sit down in the streetcar, but to stand in the back. Not to walk in large groups, or to talk loudly, and not to respond when our neighbors cursed us. Our question as to "Why?" remained unanswered. But it was obvious to us that we had to be careful.

It was October 1938 when we heard a loud knock on our door, it was early in the morning. We had been forced to move from our apartment at [inaudible]. It was shortly before 6 a.m. when my father talked to the local policeman at the front door. I overheard most of the conversation. The police were rounding up Polish Jewish nationals. My father promised to go alone and managed to talk him out of taking my mother, my sister, and me. Hours later we received a phone call that all these men, women, and children were kept in an open area. And we had instructions to pack a suitcase and bring it to my father. Hurriedly, we assembled a suitcase of clothing for him, and I was to bring the suitcase. Alone, upset, and worried, I found the place with hundreds of other families—fathers, mothers, and children. The gate was wide open. I found my father and suggested to him that he come home with me since there were no guards. Dad's reply was, "This would not be honest." And he pushed me through the open gate. "Go home. Do not worry," were his last words to me. The next day we heard that all of these human beings had been transported to the Polish border at [inaudible]. Father managed to stay there with a local family for several weeks when it became evident that he would not get permission to return. And then he took the train to mother's former home in Sombor, Poland. He stayed there with mother's family. All our efforts to get a visa for his return were denied.

On November 9, 1938, on my morning walk to school, I passed the large local synagogue. The synagogue was in flames, as were mountains of books—prayer books—on the outside. Laughing Germans and the SA in full uniform were loud, drunk, laughing, enjoying the tragedy. Frightened, I returned home. On the way I saw smashed windows of Jewish shops. The Jewish neighborhood was badly damaged and the merchandise from the stores was swimming in the open streets. The telephone rang all day. Jewish men were arrested and taken to a concentration camp near Berlin [Sachsenhausen]. Six to eight weeks later they were released with shaven heads, broken bones, and tried to leave Germany as soon as possible, to anywhere. They did not talk. But we could read the horror in their eyes. [The event] is now called *Kristallnacht*, or the "Night of broken glass." We had to move again. German orders. This time a furnished room. . . . We still hoped for father's return and a visa for Palestine.³ We waited. Late in May 1939, my father received permission to return to us for four weeks; we managed to extend his stay and his visa twice. Each time for a mere four weeks.

But September 1st, 1939 [the day Germany invaded Poland and launched World War II] caught up with us. Again, early in the morning hours, two men from the Gestapo showed up to intern my father, an "enemy alien." Poland had been invaded and Germany was at war. The war [in Poland] came to an end less than two weeks later. The interned Jews [Polish Jews who were within German borders] were shipped to a concentration camp. We received two letters with short messages dated Dachau, Germany: "I am well. Love, Benno [Lucille's father, Benjamin]." We still tried for a visa and to get father released. It was not possible. [In] February 1941, again two Gestapo men [arrived], throwing a cigar box on the kitchen table. [The box was labeled:] "Ashes, Benjamin Landau." And they left.

Before long, we were assigned to a shared room with other people in the same apartment. We had to share a bathroom with eight people. And living conditions were on ration cards, special stores for the Jews. And a year later, we were ear-marked with a yellow star. Meaning that [when] we went into the streets, we were accosted, we were beaten, and we were called hideous names. The neighborhood children would not speak to us. They would beat us up and we were very, very frightened. In 1941 in fall, we [received] notification to report to a large building in downtown Hamburg. There were 1,100 of us. We were the first transport from Northern Germany into the ghettos of Poland. We were loaded into trains, guarded from the outside. Not knowing our destination, we arrived at a spot that was neither a railroad station, nor looked like a city. It was the Bałuty section of the city in Łódź.

EVA AIGNER (b. 1937)

Originally from Czechoslovakia (in a region now part of Slovakia), Eva [Spiegel] Aigner's close-knit, observant Jewish family relocated to Budapest, Hungary, in the late 1930s to avoid anti-Jewish policies in their hometown (Košice) and find employment in the Hungarian capital. Until quite late in the war, Budapest had been somewhat of a sanctuary for Jewish refugees of central Europe, despite having its own anti-Jewish laws. By 1943, the year before the German occupation of Hungary, antisemitism flourished and Eva's father was deported to a forced labor camp, where he was killed. Eva, her mother, and sister were interned in the Budapest ghetto and—through a series of events described in Chapter 4—avoided both deportation and execution and remained inside the ghetto amid increasingly dire conditions until their liberation by the Red Army in January 1945. In 1956, Eva married Leslie (Les) Aigner, a fellow Holocaust survivor from Czechoslovakia whose family had also moved to Budapest to avoid Nazi-era discrimination. Shortly after the violent Hungarian Revolution and its repression, amid a resurgence of antisemitism, Eva, Leslie, Leslie's father, and his stepmother braved snowy conditions to secretly cross the border into Austria on Christmas Eve. After seeking refuge in the US embassy in Vienna, the Aigners were able to immigrate in 1956 to Portland, Oregon, where Leslie's step-brother (whom the Red Cross had classified as an orphan) had been taken in by a local family. The following is from the couple's visit to Oregon State University in 1998.

I was born in 1937 in Czechoslovakia, in a small town, Košice. My family was [composed of] religious Jews. My father was a hat maker. He had a small business. We were four of us in the immediate family. I had a sister who was eight years older and lived a very quiet, peaceful, religious life. In 1939, when the Nazi era started to foothold in Europe, my father's business license was taken away because he was a Jew. Living in

Eva and Les Aigner on their wedding day in
1956. Courtesy of the Oregon Jewish Museum
and Center for Holocaust Education.

the small town in Košice, all the
neighbors—pretty much everybody—knew who you are. And
as [my father was] going around
and trying to find employment to
support his family, he got denied
from most of his friends and
neighbors. Nobody wanted to
stick out their neck to hire a Jew.
After about four or five months
when he was losing his funds and
he couldn't support the family
anymore, he talked to one of his
brothers who lived in Budapest,
in Hungary. And [his brother]
said, "You know, Budapest's a big
town. Two million population.
Why don't you move your family
here? You can get lost in this city.
You will be able to get a job." So,
my father packed our belongings on a train. We moved up to Budapest.
And sure enough, in a few months he was able to get a job and he was
working as a hat maker for someone else's business. . . .

Editor's note: The Hungarian government allied with Nazi Germany in 1940.
As early as 1938, the Hungarian government began to pass anti-Jewish legis-
lation modeled on Nazi policies.

In this time, new laws came out against, discriminating against the
Jewish people. In . . . early 1943, my father was inducted into the forced
labor camp, and he was taken from us. I started first grade, went to a
public school. Pretty soon the law came out: "All the Jews have to wear
a yellow star on their clothing." Even though I was a little child, I still
remember my mother sitting in the evening cutting out yellow material
and sewing the yellow star on each of [our]—my sister's, herself, and
my—clothing. So we were marked. . . . [T]his is the first time I really
felt that I was discriminated against, even though I was a child. Every
morning in the school . . . as we started the school day, we would say

the [Hungarian] National Prayer in front of a flag in the classroom. One morning, the teacher said, "Jewish children, stand up." There were six or seven of us in the class, and we were told we had to leave the class. We could no longer say the National Prayer with the rest of the children. Even though we were little, we understood that we are different. We are not like the others. We were singled out. I don't ever want another child to ever have this feeling again: to grow up with a feeling all your life that you are different, and people don't like you for what you are because of your religion, or for whatever reason.

As time went on, more and more . . . came out of the hands of the Jews. We had to turn in all our valuables. We were not allowed to own anything valuable. We were not allowed to listen to the news. Radios were confiscated. We were not allowed to buy newspapers. . . . Jews were not allowed to go out on the street after dusk. The next thing . . . they started to gather the Jews into an area, which was called the "ghetto." This was a certain section of town [Budapest] where we were gathered. And it was surrounded by barbed wire and all the buildings were marked with a yellow star. And we were moved into these buildings. Some of them were apartment buildings. And in each apartment sometimes thirty to forty people were pushed, pushed into living in the quarters. We just barely had room to lay down. Hardly any sanitation. And there were feedings two to three times—mass feedings—a day in the ghetto. It was very difficult, very hard. No food. And also the sanitation—with that many people being pushed into the living quarters—was very bad. Sicknesses were spreading very fast. We were living in this condition.

JACK TERRY (1930–2022)

The world of Jack Terry (born Jakub Szabmacher) "collapsed and expired" at the age of thirteen, when his mother and sister were murdered during the Nazi "liquidation" of the ghetto in his small Polish village (Bełżyce). Earlier that same day, Jack had managed to crawl away unnoticed from a mass execution of Jewish children, with whom he had been grouped, and into a line of "able-bodied" men. This desperate act saved Jack's life—he would be the only member of his family to survive the war—but it also resulted in his deportation to a series of concentration and forced labor camps. The crumbling of Jack's world began four years earlier, at age nine, as German tanks rolled into Bełżyce

*and brutally occupied the region, terrorizing and isolating the Polish
Jewish population. In the following speech excerpt from his 2006 visit
to Oregon State University, Jack discusses the initial occupation and
the dire circumstances of ghettoization. We will rejoin Jack's journey in
Chapter 4, which recounts his story of survival in Flossenbürg concentration camp, where he would remain until liberation. After the war,
Jack immigrated to the US and eventually became a psychiatrist in
New York, where he specialized in helping others who had experienced
trauma, including fellow Holocaust survivors.*

We, the remnants of the Shoah, though we regained our freedom, died
there. To quote Euripides' *Hecuba* [written in] 424 BC, "I was dead."[4]
Cruelty killed me. I breathed. But I did not live. We who survived do not
separate ourselves from those who did not. We tell their stories when we
tell ours. The only difference was the last moment.

My odyssey starts in Bełżyce [in Poland], where I was born in 1930.
It's a small town or a village. . . . The population of Bełżyce was approximately 5,000. It was half Jewish and half Catholic. Like most little towns
in Poland, it had that typical square in the center of town where peasants
sold their produce on market days. The streets were mostly unpaved.
Wood houses, which lacked indoor plumbing. Water was gotten from
the local wells. The population, in general, was poor. Electricity was a
luxury. A primitive place, where antisemitism was a chronic fact of life.

I was the youngest in my family. I had two sisters, two years and four
years older. And a brother six years older. I knew them and my parents
only as a child could have known. My feeling memory is that of a close,
loving family. . . .

When the war started on September 1 of 1939, I had completed
three years of school. Among the first German regulations was to bar
Jewish children from attending school beyond third grade. The German
tanks, trucks, and armored vehicles arrived in Bełżyce on the 16th of
September and immediately started to loot Jewish shops. They took
what they wanted and left . . . notes in German that . . . translate into,
"The goods are mine. The receipt is thine. And when the war is over,
everything will be fine." We had to wear white armbands with the star of
David. Curfews and rationing were imposed on the Jews. And my father
could no longer travel to Warsaw on business. We also had to provide

[the Germans with] men to work the roads and to clear the snow off the roads. And, occasionally, I would hire myself out to substitute for somebody to do the work on the roads. Posters began to appear in Polish that said . . . "Jews, lice, typhus."

On a Friday in mid-February of 1940, one of the coldest days in living memory in Bełżyce, 600 Jews from Stettin arrived, or were deported to Bełżyce. It took them all day to travel 20 kilometers from Berlin in horse-drawn sleds. Most of these people were miserable, frost-bitten; they could barely move. I went with my father, among other men, to help unload them and shelter them. The memory of that evening is indelible. At the dinner table I saw my still young father was very distraught, with tears in his eyes saying, "I will consider that I have reached my three score and ten and life is at an end." You can imagine what that meant to a little boy seeing his father, the protector, in such a state. Saying those things. He thus faded away until he was taken to the extermination camp in Majdanek on May 12, 1942. The situation in Bełżyce continued to get progressively worse with more killings, greater poverty. . . . The demands on the Jewish population continued to increase. Curfews became more restrictive. Money was demanded, businesses were confiscated, and possession of meat was punished with death. . . .

[A]s I said earlier, antisemitism was a chronic fact of life. That didn't help. And there was a lot of denouncing[5] a lot of places. If the [non-Jewish] population had been more friendly toward the Jews, a lot more people would have escaped, and taken advantage of having escaped. That is not to say that there weren't many, many, many Poles who helped save Jews. In fact, in Yad Vashem,[6] the largest number of the "righteous gentiles" are Poles. But antisemitism was prevalent, and denouncements were ubiquitous. So, that helped in the annihilation process.

WALTER PLYWASKI (1929–2021)

Walter Plywaski (born Wladyslaw Plywacki) was only ten years old when the Nazis invaded his hometown in Łódź (Poland) and forced his secular Jewish family into a section of the city designated as a "ghetto." For nearly five years, Walter's family narrowly avoided multiple transport selections and some of the most severe deprivations due to their connection to the Łódź ghetto's controversial Jewish Council Leader, Mordechai Chaim Rumkowski, for whom Walter's aunt worked in the ghetto's orphanage.[7]

Walter Plywaski at Oregon State University in 2004. Courtesy of the Oregon State University Special Collections and Archives Research Center, Corvallis, Oregon.

Walter's feelings about Rumkowski were admittedly complex, as he explained, "I'm grateful to the man and I hate his guts." In the summer of 1944, Walter's family was apprehended by the Nazis and sent to Auschwitz-Birkenau, where his mother was murdered, and the other members of the immediate family—Walter, his stepbrother Bill (a cousin, adopted after the death of his parents in the ghetto), and father—were selected for work. Walter's father was fatally beaten by a Nazi camp commandant after deliberately insulting him, an event Walter witnessed and considered instructive, explaining that his father "taught his sons . . . how to die like a human being, rather than how to die the way [the Nazis] wanted you to." Walter and Bill miraculously managed to stay together through numerous camps and liberated themselves from Dachau concentration camp before the arrival of US troops in April 1945. Both boys came to the US after the war, with Bill landing first in Portland, Oregon, and enrolling in Oregon State College (now Oregon State University). Walter eventually followed Bill to Portland and then to Corvallis, where he studied electrical engineering at Oregon State, becoming a successful engineering consultant and entrepreneur, as well as an ardent educator and activist for civil liberties. Walter died in 2021 from COVID-related complications. He spoke at Oregon State University in 2004. In the following excerpt, Walter examines the link between dehumanizing jokes and genocide.

Why am I here? This is . . . 2004, and these things [WWII and the Holocaust] really stopped so long ago. So why speak about it now? . . . There's an old poem by Samuel Coleridge, "The Ancient Mariner," where one verse says, "Sometimes at an uncertain hour, this horror returns. And until my awful tale is told, the heart within me burns." So that's one reason for me. The other reason is for you. So that you don't ever come close to this kind of a thing. So that there shall not be any children like I was, going through what I did, through what I went through. I only have . . . three photographs of my family. When you leave this kind of a meat grinder that was created by high-tech and racism, you leave as if you were born yesterday. You have nothing. Don't have birth certificates, you don't have photographs, you have no mementos. You have nothing.

[M]y father, Maximilian Plywacki . . . was a politically active man, one of the few Jews in the Polish cavalry, [an] officer. And . . . still active under German occupation in underground activities, listening to forbidden radio from the British Broadcasting Corporation, BBC. And a very good man who was forced to start teaching both his sons by 1943, how to die, rather than how to live. How to die like a human being, rather than how to die the way they [the Nazis] wanted you to. And it was to attack them in hot blood. And he illustrated the lesson by insulting a camp commandment in Bavaria, who then beat him to death with a shovel.

This is early September (*see photo below*). This is a troop train from Germany to Poland. The sign [on the train] says, with a caricature of Jews, "*Wir fahren nach Polen um Juden zu versohlen.*" "We're riding to

German train in Warsaw, Poland, during the first month of World War II. The graffiti on the side states, "We're riding to Poland to beat up on Jews." From the Archives of the YIVO Institute for Jewish Research.

(*Above*) A Jewish man is forced to shave the beard of a religious Jew while SS men watch in amusement. This photograph was snapped in September 1941 and was preserved in a photo album by SS officer Max Schmidt. Courtesy of the United States Holocaust Memorial Museum. Courtesy of Philip Drell.

(*Left*) German soldiers mock a Jewish peddler in Poland, October 1939. This photograph was taken by a German soldier and later confiscated by an American serviceman. Courtesy of the United States Holocaust Memorial Museum. Courtesy of Valerie Rollins.

Poland to beat up on Jews." This is September 1939, and [the persecution of Jews] started immediately.

While we're seeing these photographs, keep in mind their source. These photographs, most of them, are tourist photographs [taken] by German soldiers, civilians, SS, you name it, as mementos of their "wonderful time" in Poland, Soviet Union, et cetera. . . .

Now, watch the faces of the people [the perpetrators and bystanders] who take [pose for and are featured in] the photographs (*on opposite page*). . . . Again, this is at the very beginning of it. These are the so-called jokes that these people think that they can perpetrate. It is amusing for them to demean somebody and make them a little bit less than human. And then a little bit more, and then a little bit more. Up to the point . . . you can go ahead and kill. And it is the joke. In T. S. Eliot's "The Hollow Men": "This is the way the world ends / This is the way the world ends / Not with a bang but a whimper." And this is the way mass murder starts, not with a pistol shot, but by a titter and a smirk. Like that.

And again, the faces are all smiling, except of course, the victims'. . . . And again, the faces, look at the faces. Not of the victims but of the perpetrators. Ask yourself, who are these people? What are these people? Why are these people? And the why is the culture that tells them this is the right thing to do. . . . And it's the joke: The k*** joke, the n***** joke, the s*** joke, in our terms. That is not all that different.

And all that very quickly leads to this kind of a thing where [perpetrators are] able to pose like hunters with deer. With the object of the joke. Because by now the object of the joke has lost its humanity.

Notes

1 Collectively, Jews in the Reich were fined one billion marks. Further, the German government, not the Jewish policy holders, collected insurance reimbursements for property damages from the pogrom.
2 These children were part of the Kindertransport.
3 Palestine was governed by the British as a "mandate" territory at the time.
4 Hecuba cries out in sorrow as her daughter, Polyxena, is led away by Odysseus to be sacrificed.
5 Denouncing was the term for non-Jewish individuals reporting on and betraying Jewish individuals to Nazi officials.
6 Yad Vashem is the Holocaust Memorial in Israel. https://www.yadvashem.org.
7 For information about Mordechai Chaim Rumkowski, see note 28 in the Introduction.

2

Searching for Refuge

But where to go in 1939?... America has closed its doors. Canada, South America, all European nations, Australia, New Zealand. There was no place to go...
—Ursula Bacon

In the mid-1930s, European Jewish families—even those outside of Germany—well understood the potential dangers of Adolf Hitler and his antisemitic Nazi movement. The severity of Nazi harm and the exact timing of its arrival, however, were not always clear. With the ascension of Nazi political power in early 1933, Jewish families, first in Germany itself, faced threats—both looming and visceral—to their livelihoods and lives. These circumstances prompted endless risk assessments and impending questions, the stakes of which became higher after the war began: *Where will we be safe? When is the right time to leave (or hide)? How far will Nazi persecution go?* This chapter features case studies from six survivors whose families grappled with these grueling questions and confronted increasingly limited choices as time and the Nazi occupation marched on and Nazi policies escalated from early segregation and ghettoization to mass genocide beginning in 1941. Hailing from four different countries with distinct geopolitical contexts, each of the Chapter 2 speakers encountered different persecutory measures and had access to different kinds of resources, advantages, and assistance from the "outside." For many of the survivors, separation from one's family was a common price to pay for safety (however temporary it might be), as Jewish parents frequently prioritized the lives of their children and spent precious resources attempting to get young ones out of harm's way. For families facing the most desperate circumstances of Nazi occupation with an extremely limited possibility of escape, refuge came in the extremely risky form of hiding locally. Ultimately, despite their best planning and efforts, most Jewish families' attempts to find a viable and permanent refuge failed; of the six survivors who tell their stories in this chapter, only two managed to avoid capture by the Nazis. Although the survivors' experiences vary widely, their stories reveal the intense sacrifices, heart-wrenching decisions, and astounding resourcefulness involved in protecting one's life and loved ones and finding a rare safe haven during the Holocaust.

URSULA BACON (ca. 1929–2013)

Out of all the speakers who appear in this chapter, Ursula Bacon fled the furthest to escape the Nazis and her experience serves as a reminder of the global nature of the Holocaust. In 1939, when Ursula was just a girl, her family left Germany and boarded a passenger ship to Shanghai, China. Ursula—along with her mother and father—were among the 20,000 European Jews who called Shanghai home during World War II. While these European refugees were certainly safer in China than in Europe, they endured economic hardships and deprivations, as well as the Japanese invasion and occupation of Shanghai in 1941. In the following speech excerpt from her visit to Oregon State University in 2005, Ursula describes her family's arrival in Shanghai and their efforts to adapt to life in a new culture without the resources and comforts to which they had been accustomed. Ursula is a gifted storyteller; her speech is imbued with humor and punctuated with the blunt wisdom of her indomitable parents. Ursula's story will continue in Chapter 3.

[M]y father was a very nice young man, and he married a nice Jewish girl only to discover that he, too, was Jewish. And they raised me and, all of a sudden, it's time to leave the country. We kept saying, we hoped this man [Hitler] would go away and we hoped that our dear German neighbors wouldn't turn against us. And we hoped, and we hoped. And you know what? Hope is no substitute for judgment. We already had judged the situation. And hope has . . . delayed so many people from leaving that [hope], in the end, became their death.

But where to go in 1939? My father went into his office one morning. He was a printer, a nice simple man. He lived in an old country estate with my mother. And I'm the only child. [He] came to work and found the *Gestapo* waiting for him with a piece of paper and . . . a gun in one hand. [The Gestapo agent] said, "You sign your businesses over today to the German government. You either use your pen, or I'll use a gun." . . . My father signed and left and made a great big statement about the Nazis . . . and was picked up at night, that very night, and incarcerated. And we had to get him out of the Gestapo headquarters.

Now it's 1939. America has closed its doors. Canada, South America, all European nations, Australia, New Zealand [had closed their doors]. There was no place to go except the rumor—you know how rumors start—Shanghai, China. Shanghai is an open port. My mother said, "China? Marco Polo went there, and he came back." And we had known people who had gone to India and that was quite exotic at the time. But China? We'd never known anybody who went to China. But you know, when your fanny's on fire and your life is at stake, China became very important. And very, very real. There was just one trouble: it was 1939. Shanghai and Hong Kong . . . were not holiday destinations. People didn't go [there] . . . and sit in the yacht and have martinis.

We only had three German passenger ships, two Italian passenger ships, and maybe three or four Japanese freighters who made the trips [to Shanghai]. So tickets were at a premium and the line that formed around the [shipping company ticket office] was four and five deep. But we had luck. . . . It's almost impossible that I stand here today. This is simply because of, I call it, luck. And I've been a lucky girl-child all my life, I guess. . . . The ship was leaving Hamburg, so we had seven days to catch it. . . . And those seven days were all we really needed to get the papers in order and get used to the fact that we're leaving and we're going to a place we had no idea—we didn't speak the language. My parents did not speak English. I spoke English, French, and German but, you know, in the vocabulary of an eleven-year-old girl. But I took over very quickly and we [boarded] on this beautiful ship and I make believed that I was on a holiday, and I had graduated from university and my grandfather had bought me a trip to China. You know, make believe. Make believe works very well. It makes a lot of ugly things go away.

But anyway, I had dreamt that Shanghai, China . . . was [full of] little ladies in little silk gowns with these slits up the sides. In little heels. And beautiful hairdos . . . holding umbrellas, walking over little red painted bridges, and feeding the koi fish in a lotus-laden little pond. Well, we arrived in Shanghai, China, which was called the "armpit of the world" [at the time]. [Shanghai] was exotic and teeming and exciting. My parents, along with the four hundred other refugees [who] arrived that day, were totally at a loss. It's 99 degrees temperature. It's 102 percent humidity, which is slightly exaggerated. It was always 1 percent below rain, but enough to feel like a steam bath. And we are in our good European travel clothes: 100 percent wool, layer upon layer. But we walked off the gangplank onto the land of Shanghai, which was going to be home for us. For how long, we didn't know. Of course, we all had hopes that, eventually, our visas would be called—our numbers would come up—and we would simply emigrate from Shanghai to America as we had planned.

We were picked up and . . . came to a shelter [established by the Joint Distribution Committee, an international Jewish humanitarian organization]. Well, you know, you come from a lovely home to a lovely ship and all of a sudden. . . . We didn't know what a shelter was, but we learned very quickly. It's 400 people in one room divided in little cubicles by curtains and sheets that are slightly torn and dirty. And a lovely lady with a Viennese accent introduced us to the horrors—that's what she called it—the "horrors of Shanghai," which included honey pots. . . . It's sort of a receptacle for things we don't like to talk about. . . . We spent one night in that horrible place and my father kept saying, "Okay. We make a law today. And it starts right now. If you can't change it, don't complain. If you haven't anything better, then this has got to be the best." And my mother, with a touch of Jewish resignation and great courage, said, "And don't look back. You'll get a stiff mind and a stiff neck." . . .

Shanghai in 1939, was simply a colonial property . . . of England. The Chinese were [treated like] guests in their own country, in their own city. On the city park in downtown Shanghai, the sign said: "Chinese and dogs not allowed." So, to visit with us, to become friends with Chinese was very difficult because we were just another expression of colonialism to them. Another foreigner who interfered with their country and wanted them to live "our ways." . . . There was no coming together of anything except an uneasy existence.

[T]he evenings were very entertaining. The moment the lights went out, the cockroaches, the bed bugs, and the mosquitoes attacked. And you get the squeaking of the rats in the hallways. And you wondered, how you are ever gonna wake up in the morning? But you do. And you had a father who said, "Listen, before you go to bed: you made it through this day. And you know what? We're gonna do it again tomorrow."

. . . The first few weeks, we did the things we saw. My mother . . . caught on very quickly. I'm sure her ancestors had a pushcart or something. Because she said, "You know what? The kid has a blazer." First you sew the buttons. Then she took the seams apart and pressed them and you sewed the sleeves and the lining one day, the front and the back another day. And that's how we went through our things and made a daily living. Because you couldn't even make a weekly living. There was no refrigeration. There was no cooling system. You can only purchase and store, actually, what we ate that day. We found a nice couple. We shared a room with them . . . for three months. But again, it was a room divided by a curtain. And the lives kept intermingling. And I'm a young kid growing up, and I'm actually having a good time because I don't have a governess telling me what to do, what to eat, when to think, what to eat, and what to learn. But I was really my parents' backstop because they didn't speak English. However, my father caught on very quickly. His English was impeccably beautiful. Considering what your degree of quality is. He learned pidgin English. He's six-foot tall, scrawny, sort of a Russian face . . . But he always had a smile on his face and would literally dance on the street with the little kids following him. And he would dance, you know, through the rivers of feces. It's true, I'm not exaggerating. You just had to watch your step. And he ran down the street making up Chinese sounds. And those little kids were behind him, and he gave them coppers and a piece of candy. And I learned from him that when you laugh at adversity, you are the winner. . . . These lessons went on day after day.

And when the money came [Ursula's family received 500 dollars in September 1939], we lived in the French concession. We moved into just another room, always with my parents. I always had to wait until everyone was in bed, with my head turned against the wall. I've never seen my parents in underwear. It was very strange. And then I opened up my army blanket and I popped into and slept in it. And that was my privacy. The only time I had for myself was when the lights went out.

[Eventually, Ursula's father started the "Shanghai Art Decorating and Painting Company" with a Chinese business partner, Mr. Yung.] And every once in a while, I had to go along to interpret for my father. I picked up a good, solid little street Chinese. Enough to bargain, to run away from, to go to, to find places, to run away from people. So I interpreted for him. . . .

Slowly we adapted our lives to a form of, well, as I said, a sort of resignation. . . . It was sort of a current "waiting for this thing to be over, so you can go to America." [M]y mother had been taking up alterations in the meantime, doing great. [S]he made money, and she stuffed it in a pair of socks. In the meantime, I got a job teaching English to three darling "sisters" who lived in a beautiful villa run by a gentleman named General Yi. . . . I made good money. . . . My mother still wants to be German. I want to be an American.

In the meantime, at night, I dreamed about home. When the curtains went down and the lights went off and I was alone, I went back into my safeguards of my childhood. And I cried a lot, I guess, and I moaned a lot at night because I couldn't do it during the daytime. My father told me I couldn't complain unless it would change it. One day my mother called on me. She said, "What is this crying at night? I want to know." Well, I moaned and groaned and sobbed. Finally, she said, "Look. Memories are like a picture book. When you open up the book, you look at the pictures of the past. You smell the wonderful fragrances, and you hear the voices and the sound of people or things in your past. And you look at things that are not in our vision, and then you close the book. And the pictures stay inside. Because if you live in the past, you cannot appreciate the present, and you condemn the future." So, wherever I went, I have this piece of advice.

CHELLA VELT MEEKCOMS KRYSZEK (1928–2013)

A survivor of Auschwitz who spent eighteen months in hiding in the Netherlands, Chella Velt Meekcoms Kryszek (born Rochella "Chella" Velt in the Hague) devoted over twenty-five years of her life reaching out to students in Oregon and around the US to share her story. As a child survivor of the Holocaust, she told her young audiences, "You are me. I am you. I want you to listen and remember this, because it happened." Chella's recollections, delivered at Oregon State University

Chella Velt Meekcoms Kryszek hugs a student at an event for the Oregon Holocaust Resource Center in 2010. Courtesy of the Oregon Jewish Museum and Center for Holocaust Education.

in 2003, are deeply personal and testify to her fiery spirit, as well as her father's boundless love for his two daughters. Chella's father was murdered at Auschwitz in the summer of 1944, and his daughters were selected for forced labor, assigned to a total of seven concentration camps. Before their arrival at Auschwitz, Chella's family— assisted by members of the Dutch Underground—hid in a series of houses for a year and a half. In the speech excerpt that follows, Chella describes the family's decision to go into hiding and how she coped with the confined conditions for eighteen months. After the war Chella married and started a family. In 1953, she followed her sister Flora to Portland, Oregon, where they remained inseparable, residing within five minutes of each other until Flora's death in 1987. Chella was a force for Holocaust education and commemoration for over twenty-five years. She spoke to thousands of students in Oregon and southwest Washington as part of the Oregon Holocaust Resource Center's Speaker's Board and also served, alongside her husband and fellow survivor Jakob Kryszek, as a member the Oregon Holocaust Memorial Coalition.

> *Editor's note*: Chella's mother died when she was five years old. After Chella and her older sister, Flora, spent some time living with relatives, Chella's father sent the girls to live in a nearby Jewish Children's Home in the Hague until he remarried. He visited his daughters every weekend.

So in 1938, I was ten years old. And in the middle of the night, one night in November in '38, there was screaming going on in the room [of the Jewish Children's Home]. I remember children screaming. I shared a room with fifteen people to sleep [in]. And all of a sudden about fifty children were running into our rooms, and we had to put them into

our beds. What we were told was that these were German refugees—
children from Germany. It was *Kristallnacht*, "The Night of the Broken
Glass" in Germany when the synagogues were burned. Then the men
were taken out of their stores, and they broke the windows, and beat the
Jews. And everybody stood by and let it happen. . . . So that night when
all these fifty kids were in the home, we had to double up. There was
not much room for all those kids. And one little girl was crying so hard.
She was five years old, and I took her in my arms on my bed and I said,
"Don't cry. Mummy will come and get you." She didn't understand what I
was saying. She was speaking German and couldn't understand [Chella's
Dutch language], but I tried to tell her, "Mutti is coming, Mutti is coming. Mutti will be coming to get you." Well, that wasn't true. But I didn't
know that [then]. I was a naïve ten-year-old. . . . The children all came to
that [orphanage], hoping that their parents would come get them.

So, in January 1940, my father gets married, and he takes my sister
and me home. It was so wonderful to have our own bedroom, just the
two of us, and to see my father home every night.

. . .

[On] the 10th of May [1940], Germany bombed Holland flat. . . . It
was such a fast war. [The Germans] were so strong that on the 15th of
May, they walked into Holland, early in the morning. I was standing on
the side of the street. I was twelve years old that day. What a birthday
present! And I was nervous, and I felt exhilarated. I felt very funny.

I ran home to my father, and I said, "Papa, I saw the German soldiers
march practically over my feet and there was no end to them, there were
so many of them. What's going to happen to us?"

He said, "Well, Chella, I hope nothing will happen to us, or won't
happen to anybody else. But we are Jews." He'd never said that before. I
said, "Well, what does that mean?"

He said, "Well, do you remember what happened to the German
children . . . the Jewish German [children] that were brought into the
orphanage? Their parents put them on a train so that they would be safe
and, so far, the parents never came [to get them]. And [the Nazis] did
terrible things to the Jews in Germany then. And now the Germans are
here, and we are Jews. But you know what? I shouldn't even say that and
worry your little head on your 12th birthday. You know we are Dutch. Oh
yes, we are. Nothing will happen to us. Everything will be fine, Chella."

But that night, I went to bed with my sister, and we came into the bedroom and we talked and worried about it. We were now being occupied by the Germans. [Chella describes the restrictions imposed on Dutch Jews, including the prohibition on Jews riding bicycles. Unfortunately, this meant that Chella had to give up her beloved bicycle, which her father had recently given her. Young Chella initially declared this sacrifice to be the "worst" part of the German occupation.]

Well, I soon learned that things could be worse. . . . The next thing was a notice in the newspaper that all sixteen-year-olds through twenty-five had to go to the station—to the railroad station with suitcases and clothes, with their favorite books—and they will go to a . . . labor camp for young people. . . . When I saw that big yellow envelope with Flora's name on it [at home], I screamed. I went insane. I said, "Papa, not my sister! They can't have my sister! They can't have my Flora. Please, please!"

He said, "Chella, I will try to see if I can find somebody to hide her. Please, you go to school today, and I'll see what I can do." And he was frightened; he was all white. The whole family got together that night, all the aunts and uncles and the cousins. They had the same thing; all those boys got those letters in the mail, and they sat together talking, and I heard them talk and I heard them cry. "What are we going to do with our children?"

I was so nervous and frightened to hear all of that, and I thought, "Oh my sister, what will happen to her?" And I went to school the next day and when I came home, Flora was gone. I said, "Oh papa, Flora, where is Flora?"

He said, "Chella, please don't ask me where she is, but a good person came and went to get her. And I may not tell you where she is, because if you knew where she is, then maybe one day [the Nazis] will get hold of you and would make you tell. So, you cannot tell if you don't know."

[Shortly thereafter, Chella's father was picked up by Nazi officials and sent to a labor camp in the south of Holland. He was able to send Chella and her stepmother a letter warning them to avoid arrest.]

. . . [The Gestapo had just taken away some of Chella's schoolmates and were] hauling people out of their bed in the middle of the night. . . . [M]y stepmom said, "Well, it isn't safe anymore to go to school [with the Gestapo] picking up kids at school. And I don't know what to do. . . . But you go to school today, and I'll see what I can do."

Well, when I went to school, the teachers said, "It's better that you don't come anymore because it's not safe." When I went home that night, I was all alone—my stepmother was gone. . . . Where was my stepmother? I sit in the house, in the room, and it gets dark, and I don't know what to do. I wait.

The doorbell rings. . . . I opened the door, and this gentleman comes up the stairs. He says, "Chella, please don't be afraid because you know me."

I said, "Yes, I do know you. . . . [Y]ou're the one who has the grocery store where I go every day. . . . I come to you every day with my little dog."

He said, "Well, you do know me. You know where the store is, but I am taking you with me. . . . I'm taking you with me because you're all alone in the house. Your stepmother is in the hospital. The doctor put her there for 'observations,' so-called. A good doctor. Because we don't know what to do with her because she couldn't find a hiding place. So, she is in the hospital, but she could only be there for a while. So now you're all alone and you have to come. I'll take you home with me a little until they can find another place for you." And I ran up and down the house for the last time. . . . I have to leave this time. And what is going to happen? And I started to cry. And [the man who runs the grocery store] said, "Chella, don't cry. I'm trying to save your life." And he held my hand.

I said, "Can I take something?"

He said, "No, because there are Dutch citizens that are Nazi sympathizers, and some may live across the street. So, you can't take anything, just pretend you're going for a little walk."

So I took nothing but a school book and put my coat on. And I thought, if only I had taken a photo album! Pictures of the family! And so, I walk with him . . . and as we come close to the door to his grocery store, he said, "You know, Chella, you're going to smile today. You're going to be happy."

I said, "I will never be happy anymore or smile." How could I?

"But I promise you," he said.

And he brought me through the grocery store, and I go through the door to the back room, and Flora is standing there. He'd been hiding my sister for six months already. Those were the good humanitarians among us who risked their lives to save a child, at the risk of their own life. And I flew into Flora's arms. I put my arms around her, and I say, "Oh Flora, if I can just stay with you in this little bedroom until the end of war then the two of us will be together and we will never be apart. . . . If we could just stay in this little room."

Flora said, "I hope so." And so we did that for a while. We spent a little bit of our day in the bedroom, in the little twin bed. We slept with our arms around each other, and we felt safe in the warmth of each other's bodies. We stayed there for a while, and we'd go during the day into the kitchen and peel the potatoes for lunch, potatoes for dinner. That's all there was.

After a while, there is a knock at the door, after several weeks, and my stepmother is standing there. She said the doctor said, "Get out of the hospital, [the Nazis]—over the weekend—are going to raid all the hospitals, and they will take all of the Jewish people . . . out of the hospital. They will go into the van to the camp." So, she ran out. And she said, "Please can you give me a place?"

And [the owner of the grocery store who was hiding Chella and Flora] said, "You know, I really don't have room for the two. But, okay, come on in and we'll think about what we're going to do."

[Weeks later, Chella learned that her father was in a local hospital. To avoid a planned deportation of Jews from his labor camp to concentration camps in Poland, Chella's father intentionally injured himself—by riding a bicycle into a canal—and was badly hurt. Her father's doctor agreed to help smuggle Chella's father out of the hospital.]

. . . Months went by, papa got a lot better. He was crippled very badly. But one night, late at night, a man went with false identification [papers], got my father [and brought him] back into the house where we were. What a reunion!

Papa said, "Chella, I don't ever want you to complain that you're in hiding, that you're going crazy that you can't see the street . . . because what is out there, Chella . . . all our family's been picked up. All our friends. We don't hear a word of where they are, not a word. And now, we are safe right now. [The grocer and his family] are risking their lives. We have to be grateful for every moment." So papa and I would sit together and talk about our books—what we are reading—and the [grocer's] kids come home every day, every week with five or six books at a time and I read until the middle of the night, till 3 in the morning to get my mind off of the terror around us. After a while, the [grocer] was worried that too many [people] were in one house, so they said they have to look for another place.

[After they all were nearly discovered by the Gestapo, the grocer decided to move to the inner city of the Hague. Chella's family was again separated into different homes to hide.]

So [the grocer] got hold of the Underground and they found a place for me with a family with five children. They ranged in age from nine to sixteen. Wonderful people, humanitarians. There was everything on one floor, there was no hiding place there. . . . And so, I sleep with the family. And Flora was—I don't know where she was— in another city. And . . . my parents went with the grocery man to a little shop in the city. And I stayed with that family [with five children] for eight or nine months, and I loved them. They treated me like one of their children. I hid in the little bedroom many, many, many days, many, many nights when people would come to the house. And I would read and read and read and I did not go to sleep until 4 in the morning because my nightmares were there. The nightmares were that [the Nazis] . . . would come and get me, and I was always so afraid of that.

And so time went by . . . one of the children comes running up the stairs, says the Dutch police are going from door to door, and they are looking in people's homes. They came to my door, and I didn't know where to go. And the auntie [the mother of the family hiding Chella] said, "Go to the toilet." And the toilet is in a closet in the hall. So I went in there and [locked the door], and she said, "Don't get off the toilet. Stay there. No matter what happens, don't get off." I hear the policeman come in and he goes through all the rooms, he goes to all the bedrooms, and opens the closet door in the hall, the linen closet, the broom closet, and now he looks at the toilet.

He pushes at the door, and he said, "What is this?"

She said, "That's the toilet."

He said, "Well, who's there?"

She said, "That's my little girl."

"Well, tell her to get off. What's her name?"

"Sophie . . . uh, Sophie get out."

And I say, "I can't . . . I have a tummy ache." Believe me, I didn't have to fake it. And I sat there shaking like a leaf. I thought, "Oh my god, he's going to break the door down. Then what?"

But he stayed for a while, and he went into the kitchen to sit down. Then he said, "You know when she is going to get off?"

Auntie said, "Once she gets on there, forget it." And I thought whatever happens, I'm not getting off.

Finally, he left, after quite a while. [The Dutch policeman] said, "I'll come back tomorrow, I want to talk to her." . . .

I got out of there and I thought, "That was the second time, would I be so lucky the third?"

So I had to go away to another place, and I stayed at another hiding place. I don't know all the different places they [the helpers in the Dutch Underground] shipped me to. I went crazy. . . . Sometimes it was too much to be all the time cooped up in a room. But I stayed. And then [after hiding for a year and a half], I said to the man I stayed with, "Uncle Jan . . . I want to go and see my father and I want to see if he's okay. . . . I don't hear [anything about him]. He was crippled. He didn't look good. I need to touch him. I have to touch him."

And [Uncle Jan] says, "Absolutely not, Chella. You're crazy, you are not going in the street."

I said, "I have false identification. I'll go on the tram and I'm going." I threatened to go, and then I went to the inner city [of the Hague] where Papa was . . . in hiding with that [grocer's] family. I come through the door of the grocery store, and I go in the back, and as they open the door to the living room, Flora is standing there. She was in Rotterdam. She had said exactly the same thing to the people that she stayed with because she wanted to see Father, too. . . . And so I flew in her arms, and I flew into papa's arms. Papa had a little room, a little tiny attic room. And it was the only room upstairs, and it was a very old house, a very old neighborhood with cobblestones. When you look out of the windows, you see all the red tile roofs on all the little houses all around you.

I would say to him, "Papa, let's jump out of the window and walk on the rooftops and jump."

He said, "I wish I could escape like that, but it isn't possible."

I said, "I want to go away. I want to get away."

He said, "Chella, I have to talk with you. You have to be brave and strong. You have to stick it out because we have a place to stay. It was very naughty that you came [to visit]. You mustn't come and do this again, but I'm so happy to see you." And he gave me something. He gave me courage. He said, "You know, Chella, you have to be brave and strong. You have to look at yourself. You can't look at somebody else, but only to yourself. And you have to say, 'I can do anything I want to do.'"

I said, "I do, I do."

He said, "And the bicycle—remember the bicycle. When the war is over, I'll take you to the bicycle shop . . . and papa will go back to school. And papa will start his business again, and you will help him." . . . In the situation that we were in, he was optimistic and he [made me feel] that I could do anything, that I am brave, and I am strong. . . . We would read together and listen to the BBC at night, hear the radio and listen to the news from the British side. And we got a little hopeful that the war soon would be finished. We talked about our family and friends. Who knows where they were? Nobody had heard anything; we didn't know where they were.

After five days spending the most famous, wonderful, best days of my life—those five days with my father—the next day we had to go back to our hiding place. And he said, "You go back to your hiding place. Thank God there are good people. And don't you dare leave it until the war is over. You must be brave, Chella." And so that night I asked, could I please sleep with him and hold his hand?

"Just let me hold your hand, Papa, so I won't get my nightmares." And I did that. And I slept.

Six o'clock in the morning, there was a terrible noise at the front door. A banging . . . that's not good. I put the blanket over my head. I put the pillow on top of my head. And I thought, "I think my nightmare is coming." And I hear the boots come up the stairs; they knew right where we were. We were betrayed by a member of the family that hid us. . . . They knew our names. They came into the room, pointed a revolver at us and said, "Get dressed, you have ten minutes." Called us out by our name. I stayed in the bed.

Papa said, "Chella, get up. Get up, Chella, they are here."

I said, "No papa, I'm having my nightmare. I always have this nightmare."

He said, "Chella, this time, there is no nightmare. They are here for us." I got out of the bed, I stood in front of him, and he put his hand on my head. He said, "Remember when I said you have to be brave and strong. This is it. This is it, Chella. You have to be brave and strong now because Papa . . . Papa can't help you." Later in years when I had children myself, I thought [about] the suffering of the parents, before they went to their death, that they couldn't help their children.

> *Editor's note*: After their arrest, Chella's family was sent to Westerbork camp, where Chella and Flora briefly reunited with their father. In the summer of 1944, the entire family was sent to Auschwitz, where their father was murdered shortly after their arrival. Chella and Flora were selected for work at Auschwitz, and then transferred to a factory in Reichenbach. Chella and Flora stuck together through seven concentration camps altogether and survived a "death march" over the Carpathian mountains. After the war ended, Chella and Flora learned that their stepmother survived the camps. She invited the girls to live with her in England.

JACQUES BERGMAN (1923–2001)

As a Jewish family living in Austria when Hitler invaded in 1938, Jacques Bergman's parents did everything they could to spare their children from the Nazi threat. Just before the horrors of the November pogroms, they arranged for their eldest son, nineteen-year-old Leo, to emigrate to the US. The very next month—in December 1938—they sent fifteen-year-old Jacques via a Kindertransport to Holland, where they hoped he would be safe. Respite found in the Netherlands was brief; Jacques lived in a group home for refugee children, attended school, and worked in a factory until his arrest by the Gestapo in 1942. In the following speech from his 1999 visit to Oregon State University, Jacques describes the Nazi invasion of Holland and his experiences in the Westerbork camp. Jacques was eventually deported to Auschwitz, passed through a series of camps as a forced laborer, and survived a "death march" to Bergen-Belsen. After his liberation by British troops, Jacques received an affidavit to come to Portland, Oregon, to live with his brother Leo, who was his only surviving family member. We will hear more from Jacques in Chapter 5.

This is a story about a fifteen-year-old boy. Born in Vienna and went to school, played soccer, chased girls, was in a choir. And then . . . in March of 1938 when Hitler marched in into Austria and took Austria . . . everything came to a halt. I was transferred to a different school, to a Jewish school. Different teachers, no more soccer, and no more choir.

And then came *Kristallnacht*. You probably are familiar with this. When they all—the Nazis—sacked the synagogues and businesses. Took the people out, took the [Jewish] businessmen out in the street. Gave them brushes to clean the street. Some had toothbrushes to clean the street.

So my parents and other parents got together with the official organization of Vienna, and they created a . . . children transport, or "Kindertransport," to either Holland or England. Well, I couldn't get on the England transport. So, my parents put me on the Holland transport. And then, a month later, after *Kristallnacht*, on December the 10th of 1938, my parents and my aunt and uncle took me to the station. They put me on the train not knowing I'd never see them again. I was fifteen years old.

I got on the train. I came to Holland with some other hundred kids the same age or younger. And they put me in a group home . . . and later on we moved to Rotterdam. And I got a part-time job as an apprentice designer in the factory for oriental rugs. I also entered school; I took some art classes. And then in . . . May 1940, Hitler invaded Holland. He bombed Rotterdam. They bombed us out. We had to leave. We were mostly about sixty young men and women, girls and boys. We had to leave. And we were wandering around in Holland . . . trying to find a place to live. We finally wound up in Arnhem, which is very close to the German border. There was an old castle there that once belonged to the royalty, and we made our

Like Jacques Bergmann's family, the fellow Austrian Jewish Porges family prioritized the safety of their sons and did whatever they could to keep them out of harm's way. In this photo Paul Peter Porges (age 11) poses with his mother (Jenny [Jeanette] Wagschal Porges) and older brother (Kurt Porges, age 18) shortly before leaving Austria on a Kindertransport to France in 1938. Paul Peter spent the war in France and Switzerland (in hiding and under internment), while his older brother, Kurt, managed to get to the United States and joined the armed forces. Courtesy of the United States Holocaust Memorial Museum. Courtesy of Paul Peter and Lucie Porges.

home there. I again . . . took some classes and some schooling, and also had a job at a small firm that produced cut-out figures . . . for decoration. Then things started to happen very rapidly. Restrictions appeared. We couldn't go to movies. We had to wear a yellow star, a big yellow star which said "Jod," "Jew" in Dutch. And we couldn't go to theaters, to concerts, or swimming. We couldn't work for Christian families, for Christian employers. So, I lost my job.

I got another job with a Jewish family, a young family with two small children. And I became a butler/babysitter. And one day the rumor got around that the Gestapo—which is the [Nazi] equivalent of the FBI here—was picking up Jewish people and sending them somewhere. I didn't believe it first. And then when I got home from the job, to the group home, and, sure enough, there was a Gestapo.

And he asked me, "Do you live here?"

I said, "Yes."

He said, "Pack your bags."

So, they took us to the station. And they took us to a camp in Westerbork . . . which, later on, became a transit camp for the Nazis, for deportation. Westerbork was originally a camp for refugees from Austria and Germany. And they didn't know—the [Dutch] government—didn't know what to do with them. And [the Dutch government] didn't want [the refugees] in Amsterdam, or in Rotterdam. They didn't want 'em, for some reason, didn't want them there. So, they put [refugees] in a camp. They erected a camp. And when the Nazis walked into Holland, they had a ready-made camp. So, when I got to Westerbork, they put me on the job erecting some wire fences. Since I knew some people who were in that camp, because they were from either from Austria or from Germany, I got a job in the office as an office boy, running messages from one back to the other.

And then the Nazis started deporting people—bringing in people from Amsterdam, Rotterdam, from Holland—into Westerbork. Each week the deportations started. On Monday night, or Monday afternoon, the train came in, the cattle train came in. And the lists came out with the people who had to be on the train. And Tuesday morning at 11 o'clock, the train left, destination unknown. My job then became—when every time the train came back from wherever it went to—to clean out the cattle cars. And when you cleaned out the cars, sometimes you would find a piece of paper, or a scribble on the wall of the cattle car: A name of somebody who left it there, or was riding on the train. Or the name [that] came up was "Auschwitz" and "Birkenau." So, from that time, we knew that [the people deported on the trains] were going to either Auschwitz-Birkenau or Theresienstadt. We knew where the people are going, but we had no idea what Auschwitz was.

HENRY FRIEDMAN (b. 1928)

Polish Jews could not count on robust assistance from the broader non-Jewish population due, in large part, to Nazi policies that incentivized collaboration with German occupiers and imposed harsh punishments on anyone who dared to help Jewish friends, neighbors, and colleagues. According to Henry Friedman, of the 10,000 Jews who lived in his hometown of Brody (part of Poland during WWII, now in present-day Ukraine) before the Germans invaded, only 88 Jews were living at the war's end. With pathways to emigration out of Poland blocked and the Jews of Brody forced into the ghetto, Henry's family hid within their hometown, assisted by a local Ukrainian Christian family (Marie, Ivan, and Julia Semchuk[1]). Teenage Henry spent eighteen months in a tight attic space that was not tall enough for him to stand. In both his speech to

OSU audiences and in his 2011 memoir, I'm No Hero: Journeys of a Holocaust Survivor, *Henry recounts the intense starvation and agonizing decisions that the family faced in order to protect their lives and avoid jeopardizing the safety of their Christian helpers. Despite a number of close calls, Henry and his family managed to elude Nazi authorities and their local collaborators, and they were liberated by the Russian army when troops entered Brody in March of 1944. Henry immigrated to the US after the war and currently lives in*

Henry Friedman (*right*) reunited with Julia Semchuk (*left*) in Seattle in 1989. Courtesy of the Holocaust Center for Humanity in Seattle, Washington.

Seattle, where he helped found the Holocaust Center for Humanity. In
1989, Henry reunited with Julia (Yuliya) Semchuk and was successful in
getting her family's sacrifices and assistance officially recognized by both
Yad Vashem and the US Holocaust Memorial Museum.

CONTENT WARNING: Infant death

Our "Aktion" in Brody takes place in November of 1941. About three
thousand Jewish people—men, women, children—are taken away to concentration camps. In February 1942, a young Christian girl . . . her name is
Julia Semchuk. . . . [S]he was seventeen years old. She works in a police station as a maid. She overhears a conversation between the Gestapo, which
was the German secret police, and the Ukraine police [who worked with
the Nazis] that they're about to pick up my dad and my mom's brother to
take to a concentration camp. She runs through deep snow to warn my
father to run for his life. And because of this young Christian girl risking
her life, I'm alive today. Yes. One person can make a difference.

In May of 1942, an order comes out: the Jewish people that are living
all over the city of Brody will have to move within a few blocks of the
city. People living outside the city of Brody—smaller communities, villages—all will have to move to the ghetto in Brody.

And my father said, "Once they have us behind barbed wire, it's going
to be very difficult for us to get out." He said, "We must do everything
possible to stay outside the ghetto."

By that time the Germans sent a gentleman from Silesia—he was
half-Polish, half-German—to run our farm. So, we worked for him. . . .
My father went to this German and said, "Look, I know what to plant
in this parcel of land. Why don't you let us help you with the harvest-
ing, planting? There will be plenty of time for us to go into the ghetto
later." [The German] thought it was a good idea. He went to the Gestapo
and got us special permission to stay outside the ghetto. And, as far as
I know, Jewish doctors were also permitted to stay outside the ghetto.
Otherwise, you know, once you are in the ghetto, you are like in a prison.

I remember October 1942. My father and I came home from the
field. He was called in to the [German] manager. And when he came out,
I could tell that he had sad news. [My father] said, "Tomorrow, the police
are coming to escort us into the ghetto."

But you see, between May and October, my father had time to prepare hideaway places for us. My father found a lady who took him into
[her] barn. . . . She gave him space in this barn without telling her husband or her two teenage sons that she was taking in my father.

He [hid separately from] myself, my mom, and a Jewish teacher
[named Clara Singer] who came to live with us right after Nazi German
occupation. Because Jews could not go to school . . . my father didn't
want me and my brother to fall too far behind in our education. He asked
the Jewish teacher to come to live with us. So, when time came to go into
hiding, she was part of our family. . . . [S]he was the only one person in
her total family who survived the Holocaust. . . .

The dwelling [in which Henry, his mother, brother, and teacher hid]
is divided into two parts. In one half of the dwelling, Mr. and Mrs. Semchuk live, with their children. And in the second half of the dwelling, they
have animals. We are put above the animals. . . . When morning came,
we found ourselves in complete darkness. The only light we were getting
was from the cracks that came between the plywood board. But after a
few days of darkness, I noticed that there was a knot in the wood panel-
ing. And I had a little knife, and I start working on it. After a few days,
I got an opening about the size of a silver dollar. And this became my
window to the outside. And when I got up and peeked through the window, we were up on a hill. I could look into the village. I saw boys playing
football, screaming, laughing. Here I was, fourteen years old, strong as a
horse—because there had been plenty of food on the farm—stuck with
two females and a kid brother. Let me tell you. I wasn't a happy camper.

All I could do in this spot, is either lay [down]. Or sit up. There was
not enough room for me to stand up. And all we could do is whisper, and
only whisper at certain times. Little did I know at that time that I will
have to spend eighteen months in this spot.

The people that took us in were the Semchuks, the parents of Julia
Semchuk, who in February, risked her life. In October [1942], her parents risked their lives, and their children's lives, to take us in. Marie—she
was the angel. She would send us up a pot of soup and a piece of bread
each. One in the morning, one in the evening. But she would put boiled
onions into this soup to give it a little extra taste. But I hated the taste of
boiled onions. So, I wouldn't eat it. But you know, the people that took
us in, they were not the elite. They were not rich. They were poor people.

Julia Semchuk (on right) with her mother, Marie (center), niece, and nephew. Courtesy of the Holocaust Center for Humanity in Seattle, Washington.

My father prepared food for six months, but they shared some of the food. So, after three months, we were cut down to one meal. And the one meal would be sent up to us . . . at night. . . . We would put it between our bodies to keep the soup warm so we could eat it the next day. I want you to know, after three months, Marie—may she rest in peace—never had to wash the pot because I had the privilege to lick every little drop of food that was still left.

I can't possibly describe to you what it is to be so, so hungry. My younger brother—it was boredom—he would sleep a lot. And when he was sleeping, I started nibbling away on his bread. And before long, I ate it all. When he would wake up, [he] wanted to know what happened. I said, "The mice ate it." Because we had mice jumping around. They weren't afraid of us. But one time as I was reaching for his bread, he caught me, and he started crying. And my mom got very angry at me.

She said, "What kind of animal have I raised? How could you take the little piece of bread from your own brother?"

I was hurt, and I turned on my mom. I said, "Mom, look at me! I'm blonde. I have blue eyes. Why am I here? I'm here for one reason only, because you are Jewish. You gave birth . . . to me, and that's the reason I'm being punished today, because of you. So don't blame me." But you know, something? We could not even cry in loud voices. We had to cry in silence.

But my brother started eating his bread. And I felt I needed that extra piece of bread. So, I tucked him in, "I tell you what, I will tell you a story. And for each story you will give me a bite of your bread." So, he would stick the bread between his little fingers, and I would bite in so I could get just a little extra crumb of his bread. This is how desperate we were.

I have to share with you the most painful part of the story that for many, many years I blocked out of my mind. And no . . . matter how many times I tell it, it doesn't make it any easier for me. When we went into hiding, my mom was pregnant. We didn't know how long we were going to be there. [Inaudible] My father prepared food for six months. We were [in hiding] longer than we expected, and there was time to give a birth to a child. We had a vote. By that time, we were infested with lice and fleas. We were starving. We were living from hour to hour in fear that this could be our last hour. But when the question came up to me, "What to do about the baby?" I didn't want to die. I wanted to live. And the baby would endanger my survival. To this day, my younger brother cannot talk about that past, or claims that he was not asked that question.

And what is the reason I share with you that information? How unfair I feel it was to ask a seven-year-old, [to ask] a fourteen-year-old kid, to make a decision on life and death. And when time came to give birth to the baby, there was no place for us to go. . . . While the teacher was . . . helping my mom with the miracle of giving birth, the next second, she committed murder.

Editor's note: According to Henry Friedman's memoir, *I'm No Hero: Journeys of a Holocaust Survivor*, the child's body was given to Mrs. Semchuk for burial on the Friedman's farm.

That baby was a girl. See, I will never know what it would have been like to have a sister. I'm going to be almost ninety years old, [in] a few weeks. I have to go to my grave thinking, "What if I would have voted the other way?" See, I have that guilt to this day. . . .

By June of 1943, [Brody] was declared "Judenfrei," free of Jews [after the deportation and murder of the Jewish population in the Brody ghetto]. And the way we got information [in hiding] is, when the people [the Semchuks] wanted us to know something, they would talk below us. So we could hear. And Mrs. Semchuk declares, "This area is now declared free of Jews. And it is against the law for any Jew to be alive. And anyone hiding a Jew will be killed the same as a Jew because this is the law of the land." And in September 1943, a young Jewish couple with an eight-year-old daughter, were found hiding in the forest. And they were brought into our village. About five hundred people in the village, including Mr. and Mrs. Semchuk, went to watch an execution . . . what would happen to anyone that was hiding a Jew. And I don't want to go into the blood and gore, but the eight-year-old girl—the daughter—was killed last. And Mr. and Mrs. Semchuk came home. He was very upset over what he saw. . . . And I heard the following conversation. "We have now risked our lives for eleven months. There's no sign of a Liberation Army. I'm sorry that I got us into this mess, but I don't want you to die the way the Jews died today. And the only way out of this mess: we will have to poison them." And when I heard that, I crawled back and told my mom.

I said, "We have got to leave the place immediately." So, we went to my father's place. My father's space was about half the size. All we could do is sit. The five of us. He was getting one meal. He wouldn't tell the lady that there were four more bodies endangering her and her family. We shared the food for two days, which wasn't very much. And my father says, "We cannot survive this way. You two women will have to go back to Semchuks' since you have Aryan papers." Because women could get away with false documentation. Jewish males couldn't do it because they were circumcised. "I explained to the Semchuks that you're not endangering them with your documentation." They went.

> *Editor's note:* Henry and his younger brother remained with their father for a while, all of them sharing a single daily meal. In December 1943, in order to secure more food for his severely malnourished and weakened teenage son, Henry's father carried Henry back to his mother and teacher, who were again hiding with the Semchuk family. They were all liberated in March 1944 upon the arrival of the Russian army, and, according to Henry, were the only living Jews the Russian battalion had encountered since leaving Stalingrad.

THOMAS "TOIVI" BLATT (1927–2015)

A year before Thomas "Toivi" Blatt broke out of the Sobibor killing center with 300 fellow prisoners during a planned revolt in October 1943 at the age of sixteen, he had already managed to (temporarily) abscond from the Izbica ghetto and escape from prison. Born in Izbica (Poland), Toivi's family and their fellow Jewish neighbors were promptly isolated into a ghetto by Nazi authorities after the 1939 invasion. In the following selection from Toivi's 2008 speech at Oregon State University, he describes his attempt to cross the border into Hungary for safety, his initial arrest and odyssey back to the Izbica ghetto, and his family's final capture and deportation to Sobibor, where his entire family was murdered.

Toivi's recollections testify to the resilience and resourcefulness of Jewish communities under occupation, but also vividly capture the desperation and paranoia of their situation. In an environment where antisemitism and denunciations were common among the non-Jewish Polish population, it was impossible for Toivi and his family to know with certainty whom they could trust. In Chapter 3, we will rejoin Toivi's story as he enters Sobibor and begins to plan his escape.

Thomas "Toivi" Blatt during an interview at Oregon State University in 2008. Blatt holds up a press clipping about his 1983 interview with former Sobibor Commandant Karl Frenzel. The headline reads, "A Murderer and His Witness." Courtesy of Oregon State University Special Collections and Archives Research Center, Corvallis, Oregon.

One evening, my mother said, "Toivi, I have to talk to you." . . . She said . . . "Today, you're leaving to Hungary."

I said, "Mom, what do you mean, Hungary? Where is Hungary?" You see, for me, Izbica was the center of the world. . . . And now my mother tells me I should leave? . . . I wasn't aware of what was happening in Hungary in that time. In 1942, the Hungarian Jews did live relatively peacefully. The killing of the Hungarian Jews started in 1944 in Auschwitz, but in 1942, it was still peaceful. So, the dream of the Jews in the [Izbica] ghetto [was], "How could I go across the border?"

Pretty soon a group of people, Christian people—Poles—offered their help. . . . The head of this group was Gajosz. And he promised, for money, to smuggle any Jew across the border. So that's what my mother meant. She paid Mr. Gajosz [so he would] include me in a group of Jews, which were scheduled to go out from the ghetto this night.

So I told Ma, "What do you know about the rumors? That Mr. Gajosz and his helpers are taking a group of Jews to the forest next to the Hungarian border? [He] walks with them in the forest for a while. And at a point, he'll tell the Jews, 'Listen, luckily, you made it. You're in Hungary now. Sign the letter that you're a free man in Hungary.' And when the Jews sign the letter, they are killed, and everything is taken away from them."

So my mother says, "Toivi, I don't know. Here, we are sitting ducks. We will be killed. There is no question about that. We are waiting to die. This story about Gajosz in Hungary? Maybe it's not true? Do whatever you decide."

I was thinking for a minute and then said, "Ma, I'm going." So, Ma took out a page of paper and said, "Toivi, this is a birth certificate of a Polish boy who died a few days ago. The mayor of the city is your dad's friend, and he didn't cross him off from the 'Book of the Living.' But he took the birth certificate. So that should help save you. Take this [the birth certificate]. Learn your name." The [deceased Polish boy's] name was 'Waldemar Ptaszek,' I remember. "And go to the neighbor's house. . . . The [people] who will leave for Hungary will meet there."

I remember about two o'clock at nighttime . . . [I] said goodbye to my parents and left for the neighbor's house. And there [were] about eight people and a girl—about seventeen, eighteen years old—preparing themselves to leave the town. Pretty soon, Mr. Gajosz arrived. He gave us train tickets, which he bought beforehand. Into the darkness of the night we were able to find our way out from the ghetto to the train station . . . We hid in the bushes. The train arrived [in the Izbica train station].

We jumped into the last wagon, and we were on our way to Hungary . . . but something [happened]. This girl, whom I mentioned before, from Izbica, was standing, looking out from the window, pretending she is observing the scenery. You see, she was a beautiful girl. But, she has very "semitic" features . . . I mean black curly hair, dark eyes. In Poland . . . [Slavic people often have] blonde hair, mostly blue eyes. If somebody was looking for a Jewish person, she can be easily recognized. So she was standing in the window, pretending she's looking out of it. But, in fact, she was hiding her face. But then the conductor comes [and asks for her ticket]. And she turns around and she shows the ticket, and the German conductor left. But it looked like some fellow traveler recognized her, because, two minutes later, two Ukrainian gentlemen, gendarmes [armed police officers], arrived, asked the girl for her papers, and took her away.

At this point I made a terrible mistake. First of all, I was scared. I was perspiring like someone had poured water over me. . . . I was sitting and I had a paper. I don't even know if I . . . held the paper right. Anyway, I had a paper, pretending I'm reading. And I was scared and started to pray to God. I'm fully aware that I stick out like a sore thumb because, at this point, the paper was ripped away from my face.

I look up and there's a gendarme. "Purpose?" I showed them my birth certificate. "What's your name?" —Waldemar Ptaszek. "Your mother's name?" —Stankewicz. "You're Jewish?" No, I'm not Jewish. "You are Jewish!" — No. "Yes." No. "Yes." No. "Yes." No.

I didn't admit [that I was Jewish] because I was aware that admitting that would be a death sentence for me. . . . And they arrested me. They arrested me and put me in jail. . . . I managed [to] escape [after] about six months exactly. . . . I pretended to be sick. Anyway, I made it to the ghetto [in] Stryj. [Long pause] And, there, like any in ghetto, I was hungry, and I wandered the streets. And I wrote mother a letter.

Pretty soon a German officer [named Krause] arrived in the ghetto, in my room. And he probably . . . was very well paid by my parents. [He brought with him] a "Bescheinigung," which is a paper that [states that] I'm allowed to travel on a train from Stryj to Izbica. And he said, "Toivi, now, we'll go tonight to the train station, and we will return to Izbica." . . . So we made it to the train station and [the German officer] went in to buy the tickets.

A few minutes later, he comes out and says, "Toivi, there are two ways to leave for Izbica. One way is to go in with a regular train. There's a lot of Ukrainians, smugglers, and you could run into trouble. But if you get into trouble, I must stay away. I can't mingle. Even if you have the permit. Or, in a few minutes from now, a German train from the Eastern Front is leaving to Lublin, to Warsaw, with wounded soldiers. And there's a few wagons for Germans-only. So, if you want, take off the star of David—the armband—and come in. What do you think about this?"

I said, "I'm going [on the German train]." So, we went into this [Germans-only] train and went in the compartment. There was a lady in uniform, I remember. There were two SS men, some regular Wehrmacht soldiers, and, actually, I didn't look too good. So the German officer [Krause] explained that I was just coming from the hospital and so on. And the lady gave me a piece of chocolate. I said, "Danke schoen!" And I remember the look, which the [German] officer, Krause, gave to me. I understood that I shouldn't speak too much further because I could betray myself.

Anyway, the train arrived in Izbica, and I was united with my parents. And my father told me the story of what happened when I left. You see, there were two words which the Jews in the ghetto feared. . . , One was "Aktion." . . . Aktion means the roundup of Jews. But you see, if you were hidden in a secure place and the SS did not discover you, and the train [to the concentration camp or killing center] had left, you were safer to go out, free in the street and nobody touched you. So, "Aktion" was a terrible word.

But the worst was the expression "Judenrein." "Judenrein" was like a death sentence. If a city was declared "Judenrein," it meant no Jews are allowed to be [there], after this roundup. Whole families, without any guards, without any Nazis, left for the train station. It was normal to hide. Because if you have a hiding place, you hide. How long could you hide within the floors, or in the attic? A day? Two? Three? You need water, you need to eat, and the worst of all, your neighbors come in to take the tablecloth, to take a chair. . . . And people discover you. It's the same as if the Nazis discovered you. They will beat you on top of it.

So, my dad told me that there was an Aktion, a roundup, [and] Izbica was declared "Judenrein." Except there . . . was a tannery in Izbica. The tannery was producing fine quality leather and they left two hundred workers in the tannery. The rest they took away to Sobibor and killed. My father and [m]y mother were in the two hundred people working for the tannery. This was the situation when I arrived back in Izbica and was with my parents. We were aware of what will happen. But there were different ideas . . . in the tannery. Oh, the [people who worked in the tannery] were talking: "They [Nazis] took the children, they took the babies, they took the sick people, the old people." They said, "We are professionals. We are producing leather, which is a very important for the war industry. They wouldn't touch us."

Unfortunately, I remember the terrible day. Two days ago was the anniversary of when I arrived in Sobibor with my . . . my whole family. . . . I remember the awful day of . . . April 28 [of 1943] when a rifle shot woke me up. I was sleeping in the attic. I went to the window, looked down, and the whole tannery was surrounded by guards. . . . I jumped from the attic, running to a hiding place. There were a few. Nevertheless, I was apprehended by a Nazi. He takes me outside. I see about fifty people surrounded by guards, already [caught]. And this soldier pushed me inside the group, and I realized I had done whatever I could. This was the end. What could you do? You were in a group of people, surrounded by guards. You must die. This soldier wanted to light up a cigarette. . . . So he [struck] the match, and the wind blew it out. Another match, the wind blew it out. So he took the collar of his jacket, put it up, and turned to face away from the wind and lit a cigarette.

And while I was standing near him [and the guard was turned away], I told myself, "Now!" And I slid out, simple. He looked this way, and I went [that] way, and I mingled in with the Polish Christian onlookers. Not far, five feet away. I went with them, and nobody said a word. But I realize that I still am not safe.

Looking around, I see a friend of mine, a schoolmate, Janek Knapczyk. I say, "Janek, please help me!"

Janek said, "Go to the barn!" His family's barn was not far. And so he told me to go over there. Janek . . . isn't Jewish. In Poland, on Saturday we [Jewish children] didn't go to school. But, on Sunday each one of us Jews had a friend, a Christian, who did bring [us] the homework to be ready for Monday. So, Janek was the guy who [brought me] the homework. He slept at my place many times. I slept at his place. So I trusted him. He tells me, "Go!" I go to the barn, and on the gate is a big padlock, so I can't go in. So, I go around [the barn]. Maybe some panel is broken, and I could go in.

When a lady . . . standing a little bit farther away on a little hill . . . said, "Toivi, run! Run, Toivi! Run!"

"What's happened?"

"Janek is coming!"

"If Janek is coming, why should I run? He'll come and open the padlock, let me in."

I turn around, and there is Janek with a German, "Take him. Here's the Jew." And he betrayed me. And it was too late for escape because it was a hillside, and I had seen them coming up the hill. They were too close to me. And Janek—when the German told me to go down to the marketplace where all the Jews were assembled—he said goodbye to me. What did he say?

He said, "Goodbye, Toivi! I will see you on a shelf in a soap store!" Why on a shelf in a soap store? Because there were rumors that the Nazis were making soap from human bodies. Which wasn't true, by the way. There were some experiments [inaudible], but nothing commercial. So, he meant he'll see me as a piece of soap on a shelf. And I went down . . .

I saw that my father was there sitting in a marketplace. . . . We talked to each other. . . . Two trucks arrived covered with canvas. They tell us to get in. . . . In the afternoon the trucks started. We didn't know the direction Sobibor was. But, you see, everything can be taken away from you. Everything. One thing will always be left. What will be left? Hope.

MIRIAM KOMINKOWSKA GREENSTEIN (1929–2018)

Like the two previous survivors, Miriam Kominkowska Greenstein (born Miriam Kominkowska in Sompolno, Poland) had limited avenues to safety as a Jew within Nazi-occupied Poland. Miriam's community faced a number of limitations and abuses in Sompolno (which she recounts below) before being deported to the Łódź ghetto in 1941 and then Auschwitz in 1944. After her mother's murder at Auschwitz, Miriam endured forced labor alone in Bergen-Belsen and Magdeburg before her liberation by British forces at the age of sixteen. With no living relatives remaining in Poland, Miriam immigrated to Portland, Oregon, after the war to live with her uncle who had settled

Seven-year-old Miriam Kominkowska Greenstein with her father (Zalmen Kominkowski) and her mother (Ruta Kominkowska). Courtesy of the Oregon Jewish Museum and Center for Holocaust Education.

there before WWII began. In fact, Miriam's parents made her memorize her uncle's address on Glisan Street as soon as the Germans invaded Poland. "Every day of my life, I repeated it. And when I was liberated, I still remembered the address, and I wrote to it." Miriam started speaking publicly about her experiences as a survivor in 1988 in order to fight prejudice following the murder of Ethiopian student Mulugeta Seraw by three white supremacists in Portland. Miriam subsequently served as a board member for the Oregon Jewish Museum and Center for Holocaust Education, helped establish the Oregon Holocaust Memorial, and remained active on the Holocaust Speaker's Bureau until her death. In 2010, she published a memoir, In the Shadow of Death.[2]

Miriam's recollections below stand as a counterpoint to the previous survivor accounts and deserve careful consideration. When faced with the opportunity, Miriam did not go into hiding with her family's

Polish Catholic friends. In the selection of her speech, delivered at Corvallis High School in 1992, Miriam explains her predicament and invites the audience to put themselves in her family's shoes.

In May [1940], they kept rounding up people. Beating the Jews on the streets. Issuing [regulations]: we were supposed to wear the yellow stars. We were put on food rations, and not allowed to attend school. So, I did not wear the Jewish star. I didn't look very Jewish. I had auburn hair, a button nose. I "passed." Jews were not allowed to walk on sidewalks. They had to walk in the middle of the street. There were very few cars. These were villages, small towns. So it was mostly horse and buggy. And [the Jews] had to walk in the middle with the animals.

I passed. I walked on the sidewalks. Not because I was ashamed that I was a Jew, but because this was our means of survival for my family. I'd be the one who could go places, get things—not be beaten up—and bring them home. Quarter pack of sugar, just a chunk of butter, maybe a jug of milk from the neighbors. This went on. We managed okay. We were selling things off. My parents were selling personal possessions because it was black market time. You didn't work. You had no income. Then, [the Nazis] would round people up. They would beat and kick the Jews.

Editor's note: Miriam was sent to the Łódź ghetto—along with her mother, father, and grandparents—in 1941. A few months later, her grandparents were taken to Chelmno and murdered. In 1944, Miriam and her mother were deported to Auschwitz.

There was one point . . . where I could have [hidden]. Polish Catholic friends of my parents who lived out in the country—he was a station master—offered to adopt me, to take me as their own, and hide me. No other [option] than hiding existed in Poland at the time. They had lists [to track down Jews in Poland]. Are any of you familiar with the South African apartheid system where you have to be registered? Okay. You can "pass," but they've got your number. Every Jew, every "gypsy," every Polish German, every Catholic had a designated slot, and we were all registered. So, no . . . you couldn't escape. You could try to get out of it. But once you are registered as a Jewish family with a child, or two children, when they came looking, it was very difficult. It was not an easy thing. And in the camps, there was no way. Because you are behind electric fences, dogs, towers, guards. There was just no way of escaping that. Some people tried and were usually killed in the process. So, it was a choice of . . . "How did you want to die?" Did you want to die on the electric fence by being electrocuted? Or did you continue hoping and starving and hoping that liberation was near?

[*An audience member whose voice was not fully audible asks Miriam why she did not go into hiding with her parents' gentile friends.*]

I didn't want to leave my parents. I begged them. We had . . . I had my clothes packed and we were [at the gentile friends' house] for Easter dinner, I still remember it. And I just started crying. I just begged my mother and my father, and I wanted to stay with them. And whether it was my pleading or whatever, all of a sudden they could not bring themselves to believe that things would get that bad. You see, civilized people find it very difficult to believe that "this is going to happen to me." It's incomprehensible. Can you imagine, sitting there right now, that someone would occupy this country and then—in two weeks from now—you would be branded because you have red hair or blue eyes or whatever? And that you would be killed for that? So you think, "No, no. It's going to happen to the next guy because he's different. It's not like it would happen to me." Our family is Polish; we're proudly fifteen genera-tions of Poles. We didn't live in a little ghetto, in a little town in a small Jewish community. *They* were the "other" kind. Now this sounds terrible, doesn't it? But we were all the same kind.

If I had been Catholic, but my grandmother had been Jewish, the same thing would have happened to me. You see, it went that far back. It was that inbred. The hatred. The beating. And it wasn't just the Jews. The Jews were persecuted in larger numbers. And [the Nazis] tried to exterminate the Jewish people. . . . The "gypsies" had the same treatment. Russian prisoners of war had the same treatment in the camps. There were many, many groups, however, nobody else was [targeted] for total extermination.

Notes

1 A word on spelling: In the "Righteous Among the Nations" database, Yad Vashem uses "Semchuk" to denote the family's last name. Henry Friedman and the Holocaust Center for Humanity in Seattle, Washington, spell the last name "Symchuck."

2 Miriam Kominkowska Greenstein, *In the Shadow of Death: A Young Girl's Survival in the Holocaust* (Portland, OR: Press-22), 2010.

3
Resistance to the Nazis

Other people can break your heart, but only you can break your spirit.

—Itka Zygmuntowicz

I decided that when they grabbed my arm, I would give them as much trouble as a ten-year-old could.

—Eva Mozes Kor

Although many associate the concept of "Jewish resistance" primarily with armed revolts against the Nazis—such as the Warsaw Ghetto Uprising of 1943—acts of Jewish resistance took many forms during the Holocaust and were more common than one might initially assume. In fact, historian Yehuda Bauer proposed using the Hebrew term, "Amidah," to encompass the broad range of nonviolent—and often routine—Jewish activities carried out in defiance of the Nazis. According to Bauer, practicing "Amidah" meant "standing up against the Germans, with or without arms."[1] Since Nazi policies were designed and deployed with the intention of eradicating Jewish culture, dehumanizing Jewish individuals, and hastening the death of all European Jews, disobedience and illegal activities were absolutely essential for cultural and physical survival, as well as the preservation of individual dignity. In the previous chapters, for instance, survivors described commonplace acts of nonviolent resistance such as obtaining falsified identification papers, crossing borders, bribing officials, and hiding from Nazi forces. The survivor accounts featured in Chapter 3 illustrate the vast array of Jewish resistance. The chapter begins with Toivi Blatt's recollections of his time at Sobibor and the process of planning a prisoner revolt and escape. Although the majority of the Chapter 3 testimonies that accompany Blatt's are generally less dramatic, they attest to both the challenge and vital importance of maintaining one's sense of self and one's connections to forbidden religious and cultural traditions within the brutalizing contexts of Nazi-controlled ghettos and camps. Whatever the means, sustaining the will to live and fight another day was itself an act of resistance.

THOMAS "TOIVI" BLATT (1927–2015)

Thomas "Toivi" Blatt's mother, father, and younger brother were among the 250,000 European Jews murdered at Sobibor.[2] Established in April 1942, Sobibor was a new type of Nazi-run camp—a killing center—designed for the sole purpose of killing European Jews. While not as (in)famous as the killing center at Auschwitz-Birkenau, Sobibor is perhaps best known as the site of the most successful Jewish prisoner uprising and escape from a German-run camp. Upon Toivi's arrival at Sobibor, he was chosen to join the small group of camp prison-laborers, whom the Nazis forced to assist in ushering new arrivals of Jewish people from the rail platform to the gas chambers and sorting their belongings after their murder. In the excerpt below, Toivi describes his assigned duties at Sobibor and the complex considerations and developments that factored into the plans for revolt in the fall of 1943. In his books, Sobibor: The Forgotten Revolt *and* From the Ashes of Sobibor, *Toivi recounts the daring escape, as well as the dangers that persisted outside the fences of Sobibor in Nazi-occupied Poland. Of the 300 people who made it out of Sobibor, only about 50 survived until liberation. After the war, Toivi remained in Poland until his departure to Israel in 1957; the following year he immigrated to the US.*

CONTENT WARNING: Suicide, mass murder

Now, I mentioned before the difference between a concentration camp and an "extermination camp" [also called a "killing center"]. There are no selections [for assignment to a labor camp] in an extermination camp. . . . But, you see, there were 600 people working [in Sobibor].

After a few months, a lot of those [forced laborers in Sobibor] committed suicide. A lot of those were killed by the Nazis. So, once in a while, once [every] three, four months, [the Nazis] needed a supply [of forced laborers] from the incoming transport. So, when our transport [from

Izbica] arrived, they did need some people. This was only occasionally when they took out [people for forced labor]. So, I found myself with the people destined to work in Sobibor.

. . . I will tell you the mechanics of Sobibor. . . . Now a transport of about 3,000 Jews arrived every Friday from Holland. The train stops . . . in the camp. So, [Karl] Frenzel [Commandant of Lager 1 in Sobibor] . . . told [the people arriving] to leave the luggage on the platform, that they shouldn't be afraid; [the Germans] had the luggage, and they will get it back. And [Frenzel told them] to go farther on to the alley. It was about maybe 100 meters. Farther was a little alley, a little yard where another German, Hermann Michel, . . . had a speech. He was dressed in a white coat pretending to be a doctor. He had a short speech. He kindly apologized for the difficult three-day trip. But now, he said, they are here. They could see a beautiful place. And they will be here until the end of the war. But, because, of sanitary reasons, [he said] "You must go and have a shower. Please undress yourself and go this way." He called this alley . . . "Himmelfahrtstrasse," the "road to heaven." It went straight to the gas chamber. And I wasn't there in the gas chamber. I was very close. I heard terrible screams from the beginning till the end. [People went into the gas chambers] and, 15 minutes later, they were dead. The process was fast, unbelievably.

When 3,000 people alive arrived in Sobibor, we could cover the Nazis with our hats [i.e., the prisoners outnumbered the Nazis]. But it was impossible [to get the new arrivals to revolt] because [Toivi pauses] . . . A group of people are going by. What will you tell them? Three days earlier they were in nice homes. You will tell them they are going to be killed? They wouldn't believe it! And so it happened, one of us told a [newly arrived] woman that she will be killed. And the woman then goes straight to the chairman, [Sobibor Deputy Commander Gustav Franz] Wagner, and told him! . . . But after the transfer was killed, this boy [who had alerted the woman] was tortured, as a lesson to us: "Don't talk to the incoming transport." It was unbelievable, and it was very fast. It didn't take long and 3,000 people, all of them, were killed. These were the mechanics.

What did I do at Sobibor? They called me a "Sobibor fireman." Why a fireman? When the transport was killed, mountains of clothing were left. So, most of us sorted [the belongings]. We worked around of big main heap of clothing. Pants to pants, jackets to jackets, shoes to shoes. Another group checked the pants, coats for money. . . . And the papers, documents, and books were in another heap, which later was brought to my place. . . . And I had a big oven, and I burned the documents. This was my only job.

Now we will get to the resistance. When my transport arrived [in April 1943] . . . the Warsaw Ghetto Revolt was in progress. [The prisoners who were forced to work] in Sobibor were asking us, "What's happening in the world? What's going on?" Because they didn't know anything. And we told them that the Warsaw ghetto [was] fighting the Nazis, that German tanks are burning. That Nazis were killed. And this was shocking for them. But this was also the first spark that Jews could do something to fight back and, initially, an underground organization developed and tried to plan an escape. When the Eastern Front—the German front—crumbled and the Russians were going forward, the German army retreated. They also finished the ghettos [by shipping the inhabitants to killing centers]. One day I remember Jews from the ghetto

August 1944 portrait of participants in the uprising and escape from the Sobibor killing center. The photograph features Yosef Ertman (*front row, second from the left*), Zelda Kelberman (*front row, third from left*), and Esther Raab (*front row, second from the right*). According to the USHMM, the person in the front row, on the far right could be Chaim Povroznik or Yehuda Lerner. In the back row are Meyer Zis (*far left*), Israel Trager (*third from the left*), and Leib Felhendler (*far right*). Courtesy of the United States Holocaust Memorial Museum. Courtesy of Misha Lev.

of Minsk [in Belarus] arrived in Sobibor. Many of them were officers and soldiers. If the Germans discovered in a POW camp [that] a soldier or officer [is] Jewish, they would send him to the ghetto or to special camps for Jews. In that time, a lot of Jews from Minsk and soldiers and others were sent to Sobibor. So, the Germans picked up another seventy people to work in the camp. [Karl] Frenzel did look for new people, healthy people, and he picked out, unwittingly, former Russian Jewish officers.

Now, you see, the leader of the [underground] organization, Leon Felhendler, recognized the possibilities. He, up until now, he had young people in the camp who never seen a rifle in their hand. But now we have professional soldiers. He immediately contacted a Russian officer, Sasha Pechersky, and in a matter of three weeks—not even three weeks—we revolted.

We were aware that, in hand-to-hand combat, we would lose. There were towers and machine guns. There were soldiers. We must do something to cut the head of the beast. It was a law, that the soldiers, the SS, were forbidden to send anything home, or to steal anything . . . from the Jewish [confiscated belongings], which were sorted. Nevertheless, [the Germans] picked up nicer pieces of clothing, like leather coats. They were really fond of them. So we were aware that they are . . . greedy. . . . The plan was that from 4 o'clock till 5, till the end of work, we should lure the officers [with the promise of selling them leather coats] to some places where nobody could see, and kill them there. And later, if everything went smoothly, we should, at 5 o'clock, when we finished the work, go back to the main yard. Over there we were to make our open revolt. Of course, the success of the revolt [plan depended on secrecy]. Not many people should know. So the [underground] organization—everybody in it—was about sixty people. Ten percent only [of the prisoners working in Sobibor]. And I think this [secrecy] was the success.

[*Toivi then showed the last several minutes of the 1987 film,* Escape from Sobibor, *on which he served as chief adviser. Toivi continued his remarks after the film:*]

Let Sobibor be an everlasting warning for the future generations to prevent the repeat of any human war. Keep building monuments to human achievements, beauty, arts. Sobibor stands as a monument to endless cruelty. But is also a monument for hope and the human spirit.

LESLIE "LES" AIGNER (1929–2021)

Although they did not meet until after the war, Leslie "Les" Aigner and his future wife, Eva Spiegel (featured in Chapter 1) shared a number of common experiences. Like Eva, Leslie and his family fled Czechoslovakia to find refuge in Budapest, but were eventually forced into the Budapest ghetto in 1944 with the rest of the city's Jewish population. That summer, Leslie's family was deported to Auschwitz, where his mother and his nine-year old sister were murdered on arrival. Fifteen-year-old Leslie was "selected" for labor and spent five months in Auschwitz before being deported to a labor camp at Landsberg and then the Kaufering concentration camp. In the brief excerpt below from his (and Eva's) 1998 talk at Oregon State University, Leslie describes a camp revolt led by the forced prison laborers at the killing center at Auschwitz-Birkenau on October 8, 1944.

CONTENT WARNING: Mass murder

At this time, it was October in 1944. Exactly, I don't know the date. On one occasion we heard an explosion. As we later learned, one of the crematoriums was blown up by the "Sonderkommando." The Sonderkommando were the men [prisoners forced by the Nazis] who were working in the crematorium, feeding that crematorium [with corpses], pulling out bodies from the gas chambers. One thousand people at a time. Some of them recognizing their own kin.

The Sonderkommando was eliminated every two months or three months because they went through too much. They were human wrecks. They couldn't do the job [any longer]. And this Sonderkommando [from crematorium #4] realized that their time is coming up. They got hold of some explosives and they blew up one of the crematoriums.

Editor's note: They also attacked SS guards with hammers, knives, and stones. When the Sonderkommando unit in crematorium #2 saw the fire and chaos around crematorium #4, they rose up to kill a number of SS officers, as well as a Kapo.

That afternoon, the machine guns never stopped going. All 450 of the Sonderkommando were gunned down. These were heroes, but they never were able to talk about it . . . later, I mean. Just recently I learned that the

Sonderkommando got their explosives from women [Ester Wajcblum, Ella Gärtner, and Regina Safirsztain] who worked outside Auschwitz in an ammunition factory. These women stole some gunpowder in their pockets and, through the grapevine, let the Sonderkommando have it. This is how they were able to blow up one of the crematoriums. After this, the Nazis were short of crematoriums.

URSULA BACON (ca. 1929–2013)

As we learned in the preceding chapter, Ursula Bacon and her family were fortunate enough to avoid direct attacks by the Nazis after sailing to Shanghai, China, in 1939. But they did not fully escape persecution and deprivation. Two years after the Japanese invaded Shanghai, the government—under pressure from their Nazi wartime allies—forced European Jews into a ghetto for "stateless refugees" in early 1943. In the speech selection that follows, Ursula describes how her life in Shanghai changed following the Japanese attack on Pearl Harbor and her family's forced relocation to the Shanghai ghetto. Ursula left China and immigrated to the US in 1947. She eventually settled in Oregon, where, for many years she authored and published books with her husband, Thorn Bacon.

. . . I grew up in a great big hurry [in Shanghai] and had a great time [said somewhat sarcastically], until Pearl Harbor day [December 7, 1941, when the Japanese attacked the US naval base at Pearl Harbor]. In Shanghai there were swastikas that flew from at least five buildings. We saw it every day. SS uniforms walked the street. The shadow of Hitler was always there. In the meantime, the news kept coming in . . . scattered. But the news did come in, of what happened in Germany, and in France, and in Belgium, and Holland. Of the transports of the Jews hauled into trucks. And they were never seen again. . . .

[P]retty soon we ended up in the ghetto that the Japanese created for us. And all of a sudden, we had to do the same thing again we did years before [when we first arrived in China]. What do you have? And what can you sell? How many pieces? How many meals is a jacket? How many meals is a skirt? I lived in a . . . ten by twelve room with my parents, which was one half of a room divided by fiberboard, which did not reach the ceiling. . . .

Then, of course the Americans attacked [the US conducted an air raid on Shanghai in July 1945]. They attacked our little community.

In an image that evokes Ursula Bacon's industrious mother, a refugee from Nazi Germany, identified as Frau Schoenberg, sits beside her sewing machine in her Shanghai Ghetto apartment. Courtesy of the United States Holocaust Memorial Museum. Courtesy of John and Harriet Isaack.

We lost 120 people. We dug our people [out] with our bare hands. We had nothing more to eat. And we were hungry. And my mother—I want you to know this, it is so important in life—she kept our traditions and things together. She always . . . mended. Along with her mending and sewing, she mended our hearts every day. Kept us together. Our clothes were horrible. . . . But we were clean, and we were always mannered. It's no sin to be poor. It's a sin to be sloppy. And always remember who you are. Always remember who you are. Aristocracy is that of the heart. It's that of the soul. And that we have to practice. And we practiced it every day.

And the Jewish ghetto mentality rose to the surface, and all of a sudden, we had school every day. They lowered us into the coal house. They had room for two and a cup of green tea. And there they would have a [Napoleon] Bonaparte session. Somebody else talking about Tchaikovsky and Shakespeare, and somebody else talks about bridge-building and English history. Somebody else talks about the Renaissance and Leonardo da Vinci. So, we went from room to room. . . . We went to a little school in the warehouse. We went there from seven o'clock, till ten o'clock at night. We only had it for six weeks because the Japanese discovered it and rented it out again. So we'd bring a pillow, and we'd sit down. We'd sit down, let's see, the gentleman he said, "My name is Professor Sauerbuch (?). I am from Vienna. I am a throat surgeon. We're going to talk about throat surgery today." How much do you need to know about throat surgery? But he said, "You never know when you could need it." On the other hand, he was also a great admirer of French history and taught that. So we walked from person to person as we wanted to. . . .

Sometimes kids ask me today, what did you do about dating? Well, what do you do about dating when you have diarrhea all day long? You have nothing to eat, no place to go. So, forget about dating. We had no places to go as kids. We had no playgrounds, no playing marbles on the ground. Actually, the ground was so filthy you could have died from it.

And we did survive. And we did have doctors. And we had these beautiful musicians. Talented people, but they were without tools, without medication, without instruments. So, the help was very limited.

But every day, mother had a white tablecloth on our little table. Three white napkins. A little crystal vase with two little flowers. . . . And the subject today for dinner is not how we lived, not how hot it is, not how many rats we saw today. But, what about a little bit of Schubert? Remember Schubert's life, or Beethoven, or Mozart? And that's how we lived.

And I learned that we are two people in one. We have this body that has demands, we have desires. But then comes the soul. And the soul can survive and grow and change and become part of a very productive time when you are surrounded. I think beauty has been made to overcome the ugliness. And ugliness is here to make us aware of what beauty does and can do for us. . . .

I learned the difference between a tragedy and an inconvenience. Certainly, the whole global view [of the Holocaust] was a tragedy. The senseless killing. The brutalities. The incredible moments of fear and fright these people lived through. But the Shanghai Jews were truly inconvenienced. . . . Twenty thousand people went [to Shanghai], eighteen thousand made it out.

EVA MOZES KOR (1934–2019)

The daughter of Orthodox Jewish farmers in Romania, Eva Mozes Kor's young life was upended in 1940 when Hungarian fascists occupied her village. Prohibited from leaving the country, Eva and her family—parents and three sisters—remained in Porţ until they were deported to a ghetto in Ceheiu, where they stayed briefly before being sent to Auschwitz in the spring of 1944. Only ten-year-old Eva and her twin sister, Miriam, would survive Auschwitz. As twins, Eva and Miriam were selected for medical experimentation under the direction of Nazi doctor, Josef Mengele. They were among the three thousand Jewish and Roma twins—most of them children—that Mengele exploited as human test subjects, forcing them to undergo inhumane and often lethal medical experiments. In 1984, Eva and Miriam founded an organization, CANDLES, to connect child survivors of Nazi experimentation. In the following speech excerpt from Eva's 2016 visit to Oregon State University, she describes the intake process at Auschwitz and recalls the experimentation regimen to which she and Miriam were subjected. Eva's indefatigable spirit and sense of humor permeate her recollection. We will return to Eva's experiences in Chapter 5, in which she discusses the topic of forgiveness.

Content warning: Human medical experimentation

Eva Mozes Kor (*right*) and her twin sister Miriam (*left*) in 1949. Courtesy of CANDLES Holocaust Museum and Education Center.

My turn came, and I was one of the last ones to be tattooed in that group [of prisoners]. I was number 25. Miriam was 26. So I watched all of Swedes being tattooed. I decided that when they grabbed my arm, I would give them as much trouble as a ten-year-old could. Four people restrained me. Two Nazis and two [*inaudible*] prisoners. They pinned me on a bench while the [*inaudible*] drew a needle. It was a long needle with a handle. And they heated the needle over the flame of a lamp. Once the needle got hot, they dipped it into ink, and they wrote onto my left arm. There's my dot. [Eva points to her forearm.] There's a capital letter "A-7063." You have to realize that this is done dot-by-dot as I was fighting with them. My number never came out clear. Miriam became capital "A-7064." When Miriam and I compared notes years later, she said that, in addition to creating a general confusion, I bit the Nazi holding my arm. I am sure that I was capable of it. But I don't really remember, because I was raised to be a nice girl. And, as you know, nice girls and nice boys don't bite. . . .

After breakfast we would be taken for experiments. On Monday, Wednesday, and Friday, they placed us naked in a room. Up to eight hours a day. All sitting along ledges or standing. And they would measure just about every part of my body. Compare it to my twin sister and compare it to the charts. These experiments were not dangerous. But how would any of you feel if you had to stand or sit naked for eight hours a day in order to live one more day? The only way that I could is by completely blocking it out of my mind.

On opposite days—on Tuesdays, Thursdays, Saturdays—we would be taken to another lab that I called "the blood lab." There they would tie most of my arm to restrict the blood flow, take a lot of blood from my left arm, and give me a minimum of five injections into my right arm. Those were the deadly ones. We had no idea then what the content of those injections were, nor do I know today. The rumor in the camp was that they were germs, diseases, and drugs. And that's probably a pretty good assumption.

After one of those injections, I became very ill with a very high fever. In fact, I desperately tried to hide because the rumor in the camp was that anyone who became sick and taken to the hospital never came back. [On the] next visit to the blood lab, they didn't tie up my arm. Instead of that, they measured my fever, and I knew that I was in trouble. I was immediately taken to the hospital. That was another barrack. But it was filled with people who looked more dead than alive. Dr. [Josef] Mengele came next morning with four other doctors. He never, ever examined me. All he did . . . he looked at my fever chart, and then he declared laughing sarcastically, "Too bad. She's so young. She has only two weeks to live."

I knew he was right. And I refused to die. So, I made a second silent pledge that I will do everything within my power to prove Dr. Mengele wrong. To survive and be reunited with my twin sister, Miriam. The following two weeks, I have only one clear memory. I remember crawling on the barrack floor because I no longer could walk. And I was crawling to reach . . . water at the other end of the barrack. And as I was crawling, I would fade in and out of consciousness. And even in a semi-conscious state of mind, I kept telling myself, "I must survive. I must survive." After two weeks, my fever broke, and I immediately felt a lot stronger. It took me another three weeks before my fever chart showed normal. And I was suddenly and miraculously released from the barrack that I called "the barrack of the living dead" and reunited with my twin sister and the other kids. But the happiness of our reunion was short-lived.

My twin sister Miriam, looked very, very sick, and I could not understand what happened to her. And I asked her, "What have they done to you?" She said, "I cannot talk about it. I will not talk about it." And Miriam and I never talked about Auschwitz until 1985.

In 1985, I said to Miriam, "Miriam, do you remember when I was taken to the hospital?"

She said, "Yes, I do remember that." I said, "What happened to you while I was in the hospital?" She said, "For the first two weeks after you were taken away, I was kept in isolation with Nazi doctors studying me twenty-four hours a day, and they were waiting for something to happen. I don't know what that was, and I don't know [whether] it happened or it didn't happen."

I told Miriam immediately, "It didn't happen. I spoiled the experiment. I survived." This was the [experiment] from which Mengele said I would die. Would I have died, according to the Auschwitz Museum, Miriam would have been killed with an injection to the heart. And then Mengele would have [studied] the comparative autopsies: my diseased organs and Miriam, [who] was the control. I spoiled the experiment.

ITKA ZYGMUNTOWICZ (1926–2020)

Compassion and wisdom flow through Itka Zygmuntowicz's words and her life. Before Itka's entire family was murdered at Auschwitz-Birkenau, her mother and father imparted to her profound love, Orthodox religious faith, gratitude, and moral adages that helped to sustain her during her horrific experiences in the Warsaw Ghetto, Auschwitz, and on a "death march" at the war's end. In the following speech excerpt, Itka describes encountering antisemitism in her small community (Ciechanów, Poland) and the advice and support her parents gave her. Itka came into the world on Passover 1926 and, fittingly, was liberated from her Nazi captors during Passover in 1945. Itka met and married Rachmil Zygmuntowicz, a fellow survivor of the Holocaust, after the war and had two children before immigrating to the US in 1953. Following their arrival, Itka and Rachmil had two more sons. As Itka explained in her speech at Oregon State delivered in 1997, "We combat death by creating more life within us and around us." Itka became an accomplished writer and poet, as well as a tireless educator and speaker who preached the importance of tolerance and shared humanity. Itka passed away at the age of ninety-four on October 9, 2020.

My first encounter of being hated for being born Jewish was when I was about thirteen years old. Shortly before Germany invaded Poland, I was walking home alone from school. . . . And all of a sudden, I saw a bunch of boys and girls coming toward me. I looked at their angry faces and I got scared. They formed a circle around me, and I started to free myself. But they wouldn't let me go. And I could feel punches coming from all sides. With terrible shouts. And they were saying things that [inaudible]. And I wondered, "Why?" I came [home] and my mother saw me. I must have been terribly hurt. And it was not just the physical pain. It was the emotional pain. For a child to be hated and beaten up and called terrible, ugly names. For what?

My mother didn't say a word. She took me tenderly in her arms and tried to comfort me. And later, when I quieted down, she asked me, "And what did you do, my child?"

I said, "Nothing, mother. I was all alone and there were so many of them." . . . And my mother said to me something that helps me till today.

She said, "Itkolo, your *menschlichkeit*—your humaneness—does not depend on how others treat you, but on how you treat others." It helped me a lot.

And when my Papa came home . . . he always asked us, "How was your day? What did you learn today?" And we talked around the table, and he was told what had happened. He said, "My child, I want to tell you something," He said, "Other people can break your heart, but only you can break your spirit. Your own spirit. If you collaborate with evil in your own destruction." . . .

Unfortunately, the Nazis didn't want us to be *menschlich*[3] and to survive. On the contrary, . . . everything that was there [was] a part to dehumanize us and to destroy us. To them, I was just a number. [Itka rolls up her sleeve to reveal her tattoo to the audience. She reads aloud the number that the Nazis used instead of her name:] 2-5-6-7-2. To them, I was subhuman. Just a vermin. Of an inferior race. "Inferior races" are a figment of men's imagination.

I remember when I was in Auschwitz, whenever the Nazis would call my number, I would say under my breath, "Itkola," the way my mother used to call me. To you, I am a number. You can torture me; you can do anything. But you will never make me be like you. Nor will I see myself through your eyes. I am Itkola, God's child and my parents' child. My parents brought me into this world. And God gave me the divine breath of life. And I want to live. I won't let the Nazis destroy it.

STEPHEN NASSER (b. 1931)

Until the spring of 1944, the Hungarian government had refused to deport the country's Jewish population and turn them over to the Nazis with whom they were allied in the war. But this all changed in May 1944, and Hungarian Jewish families like Stephen ("Pista") Nasser's paid the ultimate price, as they were deported to Auschwitz in the spring. After losing their mother and witnessing the traumatic murder of their infant cousin and aunt on a train platform, thirteen-year-old Stephen and his older brother, Andris, were selected for work, spending two days in Auschwitz before trading places with two other Hungarian Jews so they could transfer to a labor camp in Mühldorf for a better chance at survival. In the following excerpt, Stephen describes how he— aided by his wits, his brother, and a trusty knife smuggled past Nazi guards—managed to create and maintain a secret diary while under constant surveillance from Germans and fellow prisoners. Stephen's diary served as the basis for his memoir, My Brother's Voice, *which he waited over fifty years to publish. After the war, Stephen came to Canada and eventually immigrated to the United States. As of 2019, the year Stephen visited Oregon State University, he had spoken with over 1,100 audiences, carrying out Andris's final request. Stephen currently lives in Las Vegas.*

From the ghetto, we were going to be taken away in boxcars. We lost all our belongings. Just imagine: How would you feel? You go back home. And there are some people with machine guns . . . in strange uniforms, terrorists or bullies. And they tell you, "That's not your home again and you can never enter." [You] get taken away to a strange country to be in a concentration camp just because [of your] religion, [which] you have no control of. You were born into. [*Stephen was sent to Auschwitz and then to Mühldorf, along with his older brother, Andris.*]

Before we went back to the barracks [at Mühldorf] people started to collect the cement paper bags [from their construction work]. . . . The Nazis didn't stop us because they knew we were going to make some jackets, wraps around our feet. . . . But with Andris's help and my little knife, we were able to tear off and make pages. . . . When I returned into my barracks with this empty draft [the diary] . . . people noticed this, and they asked, "Hey Pista! What are you going to do with that?"

I said, "Well, if I ever can get hold of pencil, I'm going to make some drawings." They shrugged their shoulders. They didn't care. . . .

Then one morning, we got up and we went to work. And on the way to work through the Bavarian forest, on the ground . . . I found some sandstones. So I picked up a few and put them in my pocket. I remember Andris's face, "Pista, are you crazy? It's hard enough to walk and you're putting stones in your pocket!" [*Audience laughs.*]

Then I explained to him, "I had a plan with my little knife." . . . I carved a horse's head [in the sandstone]. It turned out beautiful. I couldn't believe I created it.

Andris said, "That's a real piece of art."

I said, "Well, I was just lucky."

Then I told him what my plan was. Following day, I took this carving with me to work, and we had this gentleman, I call him gentleman, this German officer. His name was Herr Hoffmann. He was not brutal; he was very strict. At lunch time I showed [the horse carving] to him.

He said, "My God, that's beautiful. Where did you get that statue?"

"Sir, I carved it."

"You carved that?"

I said, "Yes."

Then he was thinking for a minute. "Do you think you can carve a few more trinkets like this?"

I said, "Yes."

Then he said, "What would you like for it?" I couldn't let that opportunity go.

"Sir, if you could give me some extra food to share with my brother. And two pencils."

He looked. His look changed. He said, "Wait a second. I understand the food. But you think you are back in school, fooling around with pencils?" He said, "You better wake up! You are in a concentration camp, and you have some work to do."

Then I took that little horse's head, and I said, "Sir, the same way I carved this. I love to draw."

Then he thought for a few seconds. His look eased up somewhat. "You are a little artist, aren't you?"

I didn't answer.

He said, "I tell you what? I'll give you the extra food. And you get two pencils."

So of course, I sharpened the pencils with my little knife. And then I told Andris exactly what I was going to do. Andris was kind of happy because he used to love to watch my drawings when I was smaller, back at home. I said, "Andris, you will be disappointed. And it's my plan. I'm going to draw such awful pictures. You're not going to like it." . . .

So I went to the beginning of the barracks, near the door. There was the [inaudible] place near the wall, where I sat down. I took this diary and I started to draw awful pictures. Lines and oval shape for a head. Elementary things, even worse than that. Awful scratches. And when I finished one, I'd go to the next page. And people were curious, of course.

After work, they came down to see what I was doing. "What're you doing, Pista?" "

"Just drawing."

"Can I see it?"

"Sure!"

"You call this drawing?!? They're crummy."

I said, "Who cares? I enjoy it. You don't have to watch it." And, thank God, the drawings were so crummy not too many of them came up afterwards to watch it.

But what they didn't know . . . When I was sitting there and drawing and I saw the coast is clear, under the drawing—on the actual page—I started to write the diary. I wrote page after page. [When] I'd see somebody approaching, I just turned the page and draw again. So they didn't realize I was doing a diary. And that's how I finished it. Until liberation, when at liberation, the diary disappeared.

MARION BLUMENTHAL LAZAN (b. 1934)

Here we rejoin Marion Blumenthal Lazan's testimony, which began in Chapter 1. In the following speech excerpt, Marion discusses the dire circumstances in Bergen-Belsen, where her family was moved in early 1944, following four years of internment in the Westerbork camp. Amid the inescapable hunger and death of Bergen-Belsen, Marion explains how she—as a ten-year-old—and her mother maintained hope, and she provides us insight into the title of her 1996 memoir, Four Perfect Pebbles.

CONTENT WARNING: Suicide

The Nazis did their utmost to break us physically, spiritually, and emotionally. Unfortunately, they did succeed with many of our people. It was not uncommon for people, who were no longer responsible for their actions, to attempt to escape, even though they knew that their chance to succeed was next to impossible. But they also felt that they had nothing more to lose. The failure of the attempts [to escape] were obvious when we saw their lifeless bodies hanging electrocuted against the barbed wire. Malnutrition, dysentery, and the loss of the will to go on is what destroyed body and mind. Death was an everyday occurrence. The dark crowded quarters often caused us to trip and fall over the dead. Bodies could not be taken away fast enough.

We, as children, saw things that no one, no matter what the age, should ever have to see. I know of course that you've all read, you've seen movies perhaps, even true documentaries about the Holocaust. But that constant foul odor, the filth, continuous horror, and fear, surrounded by death, is indescribable. There is no way that this can be put accurately into words or pictures. . . .

Teenagers and men suffered most from malnutrition and were the first to die. Those who lasted the longest were the women, mothers in particular. It was their strong will to keep their children alive that kept them going. And my mother was one of those remarkable ladies. There is no doubt in my mind that it was my mother's inner strength and fortitude that finally saw us through. One day, my mother was able to smuggle some potatoes and some salt from the kitchen where she worked. And somehow . . . managed to cook some soup in secret. This was done on our bunk. I was on the bunk with her trying to hide and shield, and the soup was simmering—just about finished—when the German guards entered our barrack for a surprise inspection. In our rush to hide the setup, the boiling soup spilled on my leg. We had been taught self-discipline and self-control the hard way. For I knew, had I cried out, it would have cost us our lives. This happened in the spring of 1945. I was just ten years old.

. . . Much of my time [at Bergen-Belsen] was taken up with make-believe games. One game—a game based on superstition—became very important to me. I decided that if I were to find four pebbles of about the same size and shape, that that would mean that the four members of my family would all survive: My mother, my father, my brother, and I. It was a torturous, painful, very difficult game to play. What if I couldn't find the third or fourth pebble? Might that mean that one or two of my family members would not survive? Nevertheless, this game gave me something to hold on to. Some distant hope. . . .

[*Question: "Did you ever find your pebbles?"*]

I always found my four pebbles. I made it my business to find them. I cheated all the time. When I found them, I put them in a safe place so the next time I would search for them, if I couldn't find the third one or that fourth one, I knew exactly where to go and pick them up. Maybe that was cheating, but it was my game. And guess who made the rules? You need to know that I was only about nine or ten years old when things were at their absolute worst. We had nothing to occupy our time with constructively. No paper, no pencils and books, certainly no games. So I was lucky I had such an imaginative mind. My imaginative games were always based on a positive attitude. I would search for a piece of glass, a piece of a mirror—whatever I could find—on the dirt ground in Bergen-Belsen. And when the sun would shine—that didn't happen nearly often enough in that part of Germany . . . but I knew that the sun would always come out. And when it did, that little piece of glass would cast a reflection onto the ground. And that little wriggly reflection, it became my pet. As long as the sun would shine, I would have my pet. My pet would never ever die. I would also imagine that one day I would once again have my three Bs. And these three B's represent our everyday comfort and necessities that we all take so much for granted. The first B represented a bed. I knew that someday I once again would have my very own bed with a real mattress, clean sheets, and enough blankets to keep me warm. The second B represented a bath: warm water, soap, clean towels. And with that would come toothpaste and toothbrush, of course. And the third B was bread. I knew that someday once again, we'd have enough bread so that I would never again go hungry.

These imaginary games, if you will, they were my survival techniques. They were my survival skills. Do you know that we all have survival techniques and skills within us? When the need arises, we just have to search for them, find them, and be sure that we put them to work. No one is spared adversity. No one is spared hardship. We all have to overcome obstacles at one time or another. But with perseverance, with determination, with faith and, above all, hope, one can overcome just about anything and everything. Above all, never, ever give up hope. It is not so much what happens to a person. It is how we deal with the situation that makes the difference.

RUTH KLUGER (1931–2020)

A discussion of Jewish resistance during the Holocaust would be incomplete without the defiant voice of Ruth Kluger. In her widely acclaimed memoir, Still Alive: A Holocaust Girlhood Remembered, *Ruth provides an unflinchingly honest chronicle of her childhood in Vienna under Nazi rule, as well as her internment in Theresienstadt and Auschwitz. Her reflections routinely challenge common tropes about survival in the camps, daring readers of her memoir to "rearrange a lot of furniture in their inner museum of the Holocaust" to make room for the contradictions and bitter truths of her experiences. Unapologetically critical of the mainstream culture of Holocaust memorialization, Ruth refused to register as a survivor with the US Holocaust Memorial Museum and requested for her poems to be removed from displays at Auschwitz. In 2013, Professor Kluger visited Oregon State University to speak about the relationship between the Holocaust and literature, a topic that was prompted by an earlier interaction with a young woman who awkwardly exclaimed that she "loved the Holocaust." Understanding that the woman meant that she enjoyed reading about the Holocaust, Ruth still wondered, "Should [the young woman] love to read about the Holocaust? Should we in any shape or form feel positive and empowered or even cathartically purged when we contemplate the extinction of a people?" Ruth's answer to this question is, unsurprisingly, nuanced and contradictory. In the speech excerpt below, she explores the complex topic and touches on the personal significance of education and poetry, which she refers to as "stabilizing life-savers" during her time of incarceration by the Nazis.*

Literature, the written word, script, scripture, as I came to know it, consisted thus of opposites. And I continued to think of it that way. The high-minded type was the one that I lived by, struggled to find, to memorize, even to put to use by composing poems. The other was out to kill me, as I had first vaguely surmised, and later found out to be true.

Its ultimate expression, I think, was the tattooed Auschwitz number. The most obscene kind of writing that ever was. And which we, its victims—those of us who survived—managed to turn into its opposite. A kind of ineradicable memorial. . . .

When I arrived at the camp, Theresienstadt—which was called a ghetto at the time and is now quite correctly considered a concentration camp—it was much harder to find something to read than it had been in Vienna. There were few books, and accordingly, they were highly valued, treated with care and passed from hand to hand. Regular instruction for the children of Theresienstadt was illegal. But as the place was brimful of the men and women of the Jewish intelligentsia of Europe, we could occasionally sit at their feet and listen to them to discuss culture with a capital "C." I remember an art historian who had a volume with reproductions of famous paintings, which he showed and explained to us one evening. It was just one evening. But for the first time, I learned something about art and have some unforgettable memories of that book and those pictures. And I visited an old lady in an overcrowded room, where she lived, who tried to teach me how to read poems correctly. And sometimes a mother of one of the girls in the children's quarter, which was my home in Theresienstadt, would sit at the communal table in our room and instruct her daughter in ancient Greek history. I sat down next to her without asking permission. And she let me pick up a few hors d'oeuvres of Western civilization. Fragments of school learning. All of this was voluntary and unorganized. When one of the men in German uniform appeared, we had to stop immediately. And whatever bits of printed paper we had been studying had to disappear. It was hardly a way to learn something for passing an exam, but it made learning seem exciting. In addition, I was still incessantly composing poems, which dealt with the prospect of getting out of this prison, seeing the real world, especially "Eretz Israel," which didn't exist as a state to be sure, but which we talked and heard about.

. . .

In the spring of 1944, we were deported to what was arguably the worst place human beings ever built—Auschwitz-Birkenau. Quite appropriately, there were absolutely no books to be had there. I had a head full of poems I knew by heart, and I kept reciting them aloud in a half-voice or silently. They were stabilizing lifesavers in a place that seemed to have fallen off the edge of the earth, the antechamber of death. But I don't want to describe Auschwitz to you. You have heard, seen descriptions of it. I want to talk about writing.

It was there that I first came upon another kind of obscenity, as I understand it. The satirical kind. And it was in the form of proverbs, ominous [?] sayings. The context turned them around into their opposite. The most famous of them is of course, "Arbeit macht frei." "Labor liber-ates." The sign at the entrance to the camp Auschwitz. The second most famous one is probably the one decorating the camp, Buch-enwald: "Jedem das Seine." "To

Ruth Kluger addresses the audience at Oregon State University in 2013. Image Courtesy of Oregon State University Special Collections and Archives Research Center, Corvallis, Oregon.

each his own." But there were many others, written in large letters on the cross beams of our barracks. I used to stare in cold desperation at nonsense like "Speech is silver, silence is gold." And, in utter disbelief, at "Live and let live." . . . I looked at these "pearls of wisdom" every day, purported by their creators as pearls of wisdom and guides to a good life, as proverbs are supposed to be. Given the reality of the place where they were inscribed, they stood exposed as absolute lies. Since then, I cannot hear any of these German proverbs without feeling nauseated because I see their cynical application in the death factory of an exter-mination camp.

However, as I said just before, the ultimate of obscene writing, as I see it, was the tattooed ID number on the left arm. Mine was A-3537. The A was an abbreviation for a higher number, meaning that some other victim, now dead, had been 3537 without the "A." Hence the "A" was a stenographic sign for many previous killings. Our skins made it unnecessary for the Nazis to produce dog tags for us. I had been a proud reader of the written word, and instead I was now turned into material on which someone else could write, could read what was written. A surface for black ink.

Through the portentous help of another woman prisoner, whom I didn't know at all, I succeeded in lying about my age, adding three years to my actual age of twelve, and thus managed to join a group of grown women who were sent to a forced labor camp, Christianstadt, part of the larger camp, Gross-Rosen in lower Silesia, where I survived. In late fall of 1944, my mother, who worked in the local munitions factory—I worked somewhere else—she asked a civilian employee who pitied her and wanted to help her in some way if he would bring her a book for her daughter, who loved to read. She told me that the request surprised him. But he promised to procure something. I had no hopes. I thought, "He'll forget." Or if he remembers, it will be something like the stupid romances which the female Nazi guards read [audience laughs] and which, occasionally, circulated among the prisoners, brought in by the Jewish women who had the coveted job of serving as cleaning women. During the summer I had read two of those romances, and it had been months since I'd seen a printed page.

My mother's coworker kept his promise. The very next evening, she came back with a book, looking a little disappointed and apologetic. She said it wasn't much of anything. And indeed it was just an old and torn school book, a reader of sorts without the cover, and with some missing pages. It consisted of texts fit for high school students. I was on cloud nine. The gift surpassed my expectations. My one and own door had opened again.

Of the individual texts, I remember only one. It was a part of Goethe's *Faust*, very well known in German, but unknown to me at the time. It dealt with the ice of winter and the thawing of the ice, and the joy of the town population, who can leave their narrow houses and walk in the sun. I suddenly realized what an impact truly great poetry can have on one's life. At that time I was half-crazy with hunger, eating potato peels, which we roasted with stolen wood, and didn't eat raw only because they can cause diarrhea. There was no end to the cold. At night, when I just had gotten a little warmed up in my bed of straw, I had to get up and stand in rows of five and go to work. And here was this poem which equates cold and imprisonment, and speaks of the resurrection—it's an Easter poem—of ordinary people not in religious terms, but in the terms of

the rotation of the seasons. For the people come out of the imprisonment that winter imposes on them by keeping them at home, and they
come out simply to enjoy the sunshine. To this day, I can viscerally feel
the relationship of freedom and warmth because I understood it so well
when I read about it in a great piece of poetry in that one school book in
the winter of 1944, waiting for the liberating Russian army.

Notes

1 Yehuda Bauer, *The Death of the Shtetl* (New Haven, CT: Yale University Press, 2010),
73.
2 Statistic from Doris Bergen, *War and Genocide: A Concise History of the Holocaust*
(Lanham, MD: Rowman and Littlefield, 2009), 250.
3 In Yiddish, the word menschlichkeit (also spelled mentshlekhkeyt) describes the
qualities of humaneness, kindness, and decency in a person. To be "menschlich" or
"to be a mensch" means to be a person of integrity who treats others well.

4
Taking Risks to Combat Indifference

*How can I hate all the Germans [when] here was one of
them that endangered her life for me?*
—Alter Wiener

*You have to remember, in my opinion, any surviving
Jewish person [who lived] through this meat grinder had
to be helped by someone who was not Jewish.*
—Walter Plywaski

The Nazi regime enforced severe punishments for assisting Jews once
World War II began and the Germans embarked on their armed occupation of large swaths of Europe. People in western Europe who aided Jews
could find themselves deported to concentration camps. As illustrated
by Henry Friedman's speech from Chapter 2, the risks were even higher
in Poland and eastern Europe, where individuals—along with their
entire family—could be executed for aiding Jews in any way. Yet even
in the face of severe retribution, some individuals—although tragically
too few—defied the Nazi regime to help Jews who had been targeted
for genocidal murder. Like the Semchuks who hid Henry Friedman,
the individuals discussed in this chapter bravely took altruistic action
at a time when it would have been safer, and possibly even profitable,
to withhold assistance and comply with Nazi directives. Even inside the
walls of Nazi-controlled camps designed to pit prisoners against one
another to compete for food and privileges, some non-Jewish prisoners
transgressed the camp hierarchy in order to aid Jewish prisoners, who
occupied the lowest rung on the camp ladder. This chapter includes recollections from non-Jewish Europeans who personally subverted Nazi
authority, as well as testimonies from Jewish survivors who benefited

from "outside" help, sometimes from surprising sources. In some cases, particularly those that occurred outside camp walls, assistance for Jews and resistance to the Nazis was well organized and premeditated. In other cases, help was contingent and spontaneous; individuals made a split-second decision to help or show mercy. The stories in this chapter exhibit the myriad forms, magnitudes, and possibilities of assistance, and they frequently challenge preconceived notions of what assistance looks like and from whom it can come.

GEORGE WITTENSTEIN (1919–2015)

In February of 1943, the German government began arresting and executing George (Jürgen) Wittenstein's friends and classmates. George, a non-Jewish German, was a core member of the White Rose move-ment, composed mainly of a small group of fellow non-Jewish medical students at the University of Munich who opposed Hitler's govern-ment, the war, and the mass murder of Jews. While stationed in the Eastern Front as a military medic, George visited the Łódź ghetto and learned of the mass executions of Jewish civilians carried out by Ger-man forces. Through a series of six leaflets, the White Rose served as a voice of conscience aiming to inspire their fellow German citizens to engage in "passive resistance" against the Nazi government through acts of sabotage and non-cooperation. Inspired by the early pamphlets from George's Munich group, a second White Rose branch was established by university students in Hamburg. The White Rose's rhetoric and actions became increasingly more desperate and direct as the war marched on. In February 1943, Hans Scholl, a fellow medical student, and his sister Sophie Scholl boldly distributed pamphlets at a university building and were promptly arrested. The Scholls, along with Christoph Probst, were convicted of high treason and executed by beheading on February 22, 1943. George narrowly avoided capture by volunteering for the front lines, since the Gestapo could not arrest soldiers at the fighting front. George spent the remainder of the war in Italy. He immigrated to the US in 1948, studied medicine at Harvard, and became a renowned surgeon. During George's visit to Oregon State University in 2009, he recalled his experiences in the White Rose and discussed the challenges to organiz-ing a resistance movement while living under a totalitarian regime.

Within two days after they [the Nazis] officially came to power [after the Reichstag fire and Enabling Law], all the leaders of parties that were disliked were either killed, murdered, or arrested. . . . It became quite obvious to those who could think that this was a coming disaster for the country and its citizens. Those who could, left Germany. For Jews, it was a lot more difficult. . . .

Now I want you to think, what would you do if you were in this situation? What would you do to get rid of this elected government? . . . Don't forget, telephones are tapped. The press is not free. Radio is all controlled and censored by the government. What can you do to change things? . . . [T]he government censors, controls almost everything. So, in order to organize a resistance movement, you need communication. And communication, at that point, was extremely difficult. You never knew whether your telephone was tapped; you never knew whether your mail was read. Communication was really only possible individually: two persons meeting. Preferably somebody you knew, but whose political leanings you happen to know, somebody in whom you could trust. . . .

Well, a group of young students—all of them with one exception [Sophie Scholl] were medical students—came to the same conclusion that one had to do something. But what would be, could be something? Let me tell you how it started. I, like everybody else who wanted to pursue an academic career, or go to university [in Germany], had to sooner or later serve three years in the army. And an interesting thing happened: all those who wanted to become physicians—to study medicine—were pulled out of whatever troop they were in and collected in barracks as future medical students because the armed forces needed physicians. . . . Well, before we were permitted to study medicine, they made medics of us. We had to go to a hospital, an army hospital, and train to be a medic for six months. And when you live . . . closely quartered and go to the same places you, of course, find that some co-students you like, some you don't like, some, you hope, have similar ideas. This was not easy to find out. [You] sniffed at someone maybe for a couple of months till you realized maybe you could talk to them and find somebody with similar ideas. This happened to me. It was 1938 and one of my co-future medics, future medical students was a highly intelligent young man from Russia [Alexander Schmorell]. His father was German, his mother was Russian. They fled the Russian Revolution and came to Munich. And he said to me, jokingly one day, "Well, when all this over, hopefully, there will be a plaque at the door of this room in which the twelve of us slept and studied. There will be a plaque saying, 'This is where the movement continued.'. . .

The White Rose was not an organization. Not where you got a membership card or a number. It was nothing . . . but several individual close-knit friendships between a few people. And if you take three double, you have at least six already of the original participants in the White Rose. These were two friends that had the same interests . . . they went to the same non-medical lectures, went to the same theater shows, and, eventually in the course of time of years, these three individual double friendships joined together and became the center, the root, of what was later called the White Rose. . . .

So the day came when we discussed amongst ourselves what could be done about this . . . how could Germany be saved from a terrible end? Which obviously would come even if there had been no war. The plans of the government, for the future Germany, were horrible. And other things began. That Jews were mistreated, were more and more, step by step, by law, restricted from activities that a normal citizen could expect to do. Most of this went unrecognized by the majority. The first concentration camp was started as early as 1934 [Dachau was opened in 1933] and served for one purpose only: to eliminate anybody who was a "danger" to the government and to society as such. . . .

We decided that the only hope to accomplish anything outside of assassination [of Hitler]—how can an ordinary citizen assassinate someone who is surrounded by hundreds of secret police and never one-to-one or close by?—was to educate the German population into what the government really planned for them. Hoping they would come to their senses and one day would stand up.

So how can you do this? Radio is out of the question. Television? Germany had already television then, but it . . . was a very small area that had television. Newspapers? No way you could communicate with anybody [since the government controlled the newspapers]. So, the plan was made to write and print leaflets which would be distributed by mail or by messenger with the hopes that as many similar cells would be founded at as many universities as possible. Who then, in turn, would either reproduce these leaflets or write their own. That's how it all started.

You must not forget that war had started [in September 1939]. Germany had, to the surprise of everybody, been imminently successfully, conquering within a few months most of Europe. So all of Europe has become a virtual prison for everybody who lived there. German citizen or not, you could not travel. You could not escape because at the border you were not permitted to leave the country without a special permit issued by the government. So every German, whether citizen or not, lived in a prison. . . .

But there were problems that we didn't think of. This was war. Everything [was] controlled. You could not go in to the store and buy a ream of paper. If you're lucky, you could buy maybe a hundred sheets. Same thing if you went to post office to buy a hundred stamps—you became immediately suspicious. Why would the average person need 100 stamps? How do you make ten, a hundred, maybe 1,000 leaflets out of one typewriter? You can make six copies if you're lucky. If you have a *mimeograph* [an old-fashioned copy machine], which most of you have never seen. . . . How could you buy this machine? You didn't need it for your job. Your job was to be a student. Well, eventually, somebody managed to get a copy machine, which made it possible to produce the leaflets, in small editions of 100 or 200. One reached over 1,000. . . . [T]o avoid detection, they were mailed from different post office boxes all over the city of Munich, and many were transported to other cities and mailed there. Even in Austria, so the Gestapo would not think they were all coming from Munich and put everybody in Munich under observation. So, in the first two months, May and June [1942], [four] leaflets were produced . . . in rapid sequence and distributed. . . .

Several in the White Rose decided to paint coffee [shops] and houses, including the university. And in three nights, they painted, "Freedom"; "Down with Hitler"; and "Hitler Mass Murderer." These were . . . the slogans that they painted, even on the outside of the university and were never caught [for doing it]. I painted in the public toilets in the university building. I thought this was safest because nobody knew what you were doing when you're in "the john." And they never found out who left the paintings. . . .

Photograph taken by George Wittenstein of fellow members of the White Rose resistance group. Pictured are Hans Scholl (*left*), Alexander Schmorell (*second from left, hidden*), Sophie Scholl, and Christoph Probst (*right*). July 23, 1942. Photo: akg-images / George (Jürgen) Wittenstein.

[*George explains that the Nazi government didn't want medical students to have the summer months off since they would be roaming about unsupervised.*] Well, [the German army] came to the great idea to ship us all to Russia as medics. . . . It was, for most of us, an interesting experience, harrowing in many ways. It gave a few of us the opportunity to see what the Germans had done in countries like Poland and Russia, how people were treated. It gave me personally the opportunity to visit the ghetto in Łódź. You couldn't get in, but we could go to the entrance and observe at the entrance what happened. . . .

And, interestingly enough, the ghetto was guarded by Ukrainians. Ukraine was a Russian province that was favored by Germans because they were anti-Russian, naturally, because of what the Russians had done to them. So, there were a thousand Ukrainians in German uniforms fighting the Russians. And I got a lot of information from some of them. One Ukrainian officer told me he had been here in Poland only a few days, that he was stationed in Lithuania, and that his troops helped to eliminate 21,000 Lithuanian Jews. I never saw executions of Jews or others, but one day I was in an ambulance coming through a forest in Russia. We were stopped and there came a column of trucks full of people, which disappeared into the forest. Then we heard shooting, and the trucks came back empty. It was obvious to me what was going on. These were mass executions of probably Jews, or maybe some Russians that fought against the Germans. [*long pause*]

When we came back from Russia . . . our studies continued. [The] situation became more desperate. Two more leaflets were produced and distributed. The first leaflet was written by Alexander Schmorell. . . . And the other leaflets were written by [Hans] Scholl and Schmorell together. The last leaflet was written entirely by Professor [Kurt] Huber. . . . There were, as I mentioned, certain professors which were great favorites with their students, even if they didn't teach something that the students were particularly interested in. They were professors who were relatively frank in what they said. Even at risking their own jobs, or their lives. . . . And we took Professor Huber into our [confidence] . . . told him our secret plans. And he participated through many evenings where plans were discussed. *What do we do next? What do we do best?* And so on. And he wrote a draft for a leaflet, which was the last leaflet that was printed and distributed. And if you look at the leaflets, if you read all six, the last two are completely different from the first four.

I said to Hans Scholl, "Look, we can't go on like this. It's wonderful and nice to print leaflets that extol Nietzsche and Plato, all the famous philosophers. That's not good enough. The situation is that bad in Germany, that dire, that we have to ask now for resistance. Preferably not only passive, but also active resistance." And I learned later that Professor Huber gave him the same opinion. And the last two leaflets were completely different in tone and character and content.

. . . [T]he summer we were enlisted, all activities were interrupted for three months because we were all shipped to Russia. And then something terrible happened. Hans Scholl had told us that he had planned to maybe one day distribute leaflets inside the university. And we all told him, "This is crazy. Too risky. We can't do it and shouldn't do it." One day, he and his sister [Sophie Scholl] decided they would do it without telling anybody else.

So, [on February 18, 1943] Hans and Sophie . . . used this golden hour universities have. [At German] universities, all lectures begin 15 minutes after the [hour] and nobody during the next 45 minutes enters or leaves the lecture. They had . . . 45 [minutes] during which they could act. And they took the suitcase that was full of leaflets, put the stack in front of the entrance door to every lecture. Then they left the building. In fact, it dawned on them, "My God, we have so many leaflets left." They went back . . . up to the top floor and, in a spontaneous sense of urgency and joy, Sophie threw a whole stack of leaflets down into the atrium. On the ground floor stood the chief janitor at the university, who happened to see them and went up and arrested Hans Scholl. . . . [*George goes on describes the arrest of Alexander Schmorell and Christoph Probst, as well as the trial of Hans and Sophie Scholl. George also explains how he avoided arrest.*]

[*An audience member asks if George felt "that the pamphlets had an effect on people's attitudes?"*]

Well, I must say that for almost twenty years, I thought that everything we had done and sacrificed—so many lives—was in vain. That we had accomplished nothing. It was a very depressing conclusion. Now, fifty years later . . . talking to younger German students, a generation later—maybe really two generations later—I think it has had a definite late effect. Students have more and more come to the conclusion how important it is for a person, for an individual, to stand up for your own opinion. To live your convictions regardless of the consequences, which is a very un-German attitude, because ever since the eighteenth century . . . Germans were drilled from early childhood on to . . . if somebody whistles, then you stand still and obey. That has, thank God, almost completely disappeared.

[*Question: "If communication was so difficult, were [the White Rose members] aware of other resistance groups that were operating in Germany?"*]

We were not [aware], except for a small group of military people who . . . were all connected loosely with the 20th of July Movement of the Generals and so on who were executed. We had a connection with them. This group had planned to have a man by the name of [Carl Friedrich] Goerdeler [become] the new chancellor of Germany. And we had a loose connection to them, which all came to naught, of course. . . . I did not learn until now, maybe twenty years ago when a Jewish temple and synagogue in Santa Barbara showed a map, which is still there on the wall, showing all places in Germany where there was a resistance movement or resistance group—over 300. None of them knew of each other because of the problem of communication. . . . Professor [Michael] Kater at University of Toronto has written and done extensive research on youth under Hitler. And the book was *Hitler Jugend* (*Hitler Youth*). But he has found material of young Germans in their late teens and early twenties. What they had done against Nazis is a hundred times more than we in the White Rose ever did.

KNUD DYBY (1915–2011)

Knud (Dyring) Dyby was part of a remarkable effort that saved the lives of nearly all the 8,000 Jews in Denmark. As a non-Jewish police officer in Denmark during German occupation, Knud worked closely with the Danish Resistance and safeguarded a large-scale operation to smuggle thousands of Jews—as well as others targeted by the Nazis—to Sweden via fishing boats before they could be deported to concentration camps and killing centers. This rescue mission was predicated, in large part, upon the political will of the Swedish government, which stood out among other nations at the time by offering Jews refuge.[1] Despite being pursued by German authorities for his acts of resistance and sabotage, Knud continued transports—of people and information for the Danish Resistance—to Sweden until the war's end. In 1957, Knud immigrated to the US and settled in the Bay Area. In recognition of his role in the Danish rescue, Knud was officially recognized as one of the Righteous Among the Nations by Yad Vashem in 2004. In his 1996 speech at Oregon State University, Knud describes his extensive involvement in the Danish Resistance movement and the impressive level of participation from non-Jewish Danes to assist their Jewish neighbors.

We, who are still alive and able, owe it to society to tell our stories because society must learn from the past mistakes. . . . I was able to help some Jewish families, many Danish saboteurs, politicians, German deserters, Baltic refugees, and British and American airmen to avoid being captured by Gestapo by taking them by boats to freedom in neighboring country, Sweden. I was just fortunate enough to be at the right place, at the right time. . . . I never considered myself being a hero for what I did. However, I'm speaking for friends who were not as fortunate as I, but [were] caught and suffered and died in the hands of Gestapo.

I was born in 1915 and grew up in Randers, in Jutland, in Denmark. My father owned a printing company, and I chose to become a printer and advertising man. When I was twenty, I had to appear in front of a military commission, a selection board for compulsory service. It was a custom in Denmark to choose two good-looking fellows from each county to serve as Guardsmen for the King's Guard regiment. It must have been a pretty bad year for good looks [audience laughs], because I was chosen as a guardsman for King Christian X. . . .

On the 9th of April 1940, early in the morning, I woke up in Jutland to the noise of hundreds of German airplanes over our sleepy heads. Instead of bombs, we received fliers of cheap paper with the message—in faulty Danish—that we were protected and that [the Germans] would respect our king, our government, army, navy, police, and judicial system.

To resist in the flat and small country of Denmark, against the enormous German war machine, would have been a dramatic farce. Whereas Norway, invaded the day after, fought bravely for some time and consequently suffered a great deal. From 1940 to 1943, it was relatively easy in Denmark. The Germans needed all the products they could put their hands on. And they needed the railroads for the transportation of their troops up to Norway. Almost everything [was] being expropriated by the hungry occupiers, including paper.

There wasn't much work in the printing industry, and I had to look for another job. The State Police Department was short on manpower . . . in that difficult situation. And they had an opening, especially for former Guardsmen. I applied and was accepted after a training course at the police academy. We were supposed to keep the generally unhappy [Danish] population from [engaging in] anti-German behavior and from sabotage of factories. They were forced to work for the Germans while [the Germans], as occupiers, robbed us, not only of our merchandise, but most of all, of our independent Danish pride and dignity. It was quite a balancing act to be a police officer: On one hand, [to] make the Nazis believe that we wanted to keep peace and order. And on the other hand, [to] assist the fast-growing resistance. Some of us [Danish policemen] were able to supply members of the underground with weapons and instructions on their use. It was small acts of sabotage to begin with. Like, we were driving in a police car down the street, and we would throw bricks through the windows of a Nazi office. . . . But then, innocently, we

Photograph of Knud Dyby, ca. 1945. Courtesy of the United States Holocaust Memorial Museum Collection. Gift of Knud Dyby.

would drive back into the police station and report that "some irresponsible individuals had made a silly act of anti-German behavior." And somehow one of the very few "Quislings"[2] in Denmark reported me to the German commander, General Hermann von Hanneken.

In August 1943, the Germans interned the Danish army and navy. And the army resisted a little bit. But the navy personnel managed to sink most of their own ships before the Germans could get them. Even the submarines went down to the bottom of the harbor. But this time to stay there, and not come up again. On Amelienborg Castle, the guards defended themselves and gave the Germans a heavy loss until the Germans decided that they really did not want the king as a prisoner. But as the anti-German sabotage and resistance grew in Denmark, Hitler and [Heinrich] Himmler became upset over the happenings in the otherwise favored protectorate to the north. And they demanded a different, more co-operative Danish government and much tougher laws against the resistance. . . . [T]hat lasted about eight days until the Germans realized that in Denmark, they would have to forget some of their demands and get the country back to normal. And they gave up.

But now [in the fall of 1943] they sent trained police troops from Germany up to help the Gestapo arrest the Danish Jews and the Danish communists and send them to concentration camps. A German friend of Denmark—a naval officer, [Georg] Duckwitz—had warned the Danish government officials about the raid.[3] And the news spread all over town, just like wildfire. That day . . . the Jews in Denmark were warned . . . by their neighbors, to leave their homes. And they were invited into the homes of neighbors, churches, and farms. Hundreds were evacuated by ambulances and brought into hospitals where they were put to bed in various wards, even if they were perfectly well. One of the nurses asked the doctor, [Jørgen] Kieler . . . what kind of sickness she should use for the hospital record and the doctor answered smilingly, "Why don't you put 'German measles'?" [*The audience at OSU erupted with laughter.*]

The Gestapo had obtained most of the addresses of the Jewish families by stealing their names from the synagogue in Copenhagen. However, with all the manpower and the people coming up from Germany—all the police troops—they were not able to catch more than 350 [Danish Jews]. The oldest, a lady of 102 years old, and the youngest, a kid that was 2 years old. On October 1 [1943], [on the Jewish holiday of] Rosh Hashanah, we at the police station at Frederiksberg heard of the German raids. And I wasn't surprised when my colleague Frej [Jessen Petersen] asked me to assist one of his neighbor families of Jews to flee to Sweden. Frej and I were both Guardsmen. And he knew that I had earlier helped some saboteurs out of Copenhagen and North Harbor.

We set up a meeting place at a local chocolate shop. And in the evening, I met a few families. . . . And with all their suitcases and boxes, they looked like tourists going for a long trip. They had plenty of warm clothes on, and with the baggage they had, it would not be hard for Gestapo men to see what . . . was going to happen. We split up in smaller groups—the contact people [did]—so that we could arrive at the same station about the same time, using buses and streetcars until we came close to the harbor. Or . . . we could hire some very good and discreet taxi drivers until we came to a point, not too far from the harbor, where we huddled together in small wooden shacks where the commercial fishermen kept their tools and their nets.

Together with one on my fisher-friends by the name of [Bernhard] Ingemann-Andersen, we argued and negotiated with the other fishing skippers to get our Jews on board and on the way first. Some of the skippers were only paid enough to take care of the fuel and their necessities. We learned to hold down the cost, and we learned to be sure that the boats had a full load of passengers before they took off. Fortunately, the Danish Police Department had the control of the harbors . . . and also control of the documents required to do fishing. So, only the fishing vessels and their commercial vessels could sail. . . . [M]y police colleagues in the harbor could tell us about the traffic of the German Navy patrol boats so we could avoid them. If they went north, we went south, et cetera. We had scouts at the entrance to the harbors who warned us every time a Gestapo unit was near. And we were extremely nervous every time we sent a boat away. And we were very happy when we, in the morning, had a report that the fishing boat was safely back at the dock. The weather in October is normally bad . . . and the evenings are quite dark. And this is one of the reasons that the Danish, at many different places and in many different boats, and also some larger ships, were able to rescue more than 7,000 Jews until they, in May 1945, could come back to Denmark and to their homes and their jobs and their businesses that had been waiting for them.

Every time I came back to the police station, there were secretly phone calls for more people who themselves had friends who needed a trip on our boats. Meeting Jews whom you had never met, or even heard of, before the fall of 1943 was a strange experience. Sometimes not even catching their names or their family relationships. It was immaterial to the mission that we had in front of us, the one we set forward to accomplish. Outside our meeting place at a chocolate shop, German soldiers, three together, steel-helmeted and loaded with machine guns in their arms, patrolled the streets, night and day. But more upsetting than the uniformed soldiers were . . . the Gestapo and their helpers in civilian clothes. Because of their brutal ways and surprise arrests, usually followed by painful interrogations and indiscriminate killings, we never knew whose names were in their little black books.

In the action of helping, I'm reminded of my deceased friend, Otto Springer from Prague—also a recognized rescuer—who [said], "The hand of compassion was sometimes faster than the calculus of reason." Surely, we felt uneasy and apprehensive about the refugees. But then you felt their compassion and strength. And you knew that they were the ones who had to flee their previous comfortable existence, their homes, and businesses, for a completely unknown future. We saw their confidence in us, that we were able to help them. Their words, their eyes, and their nervous hands on our arms blew away any kind of hesitation you might have had. The only thing, which counted was to guide these unfortunate [fellow citizens] away from the Nazi madmen, from arrest, and from Germany's deadly concentration camps. None of the boats I sent over with Jews were caught. But two fishing skippers were caught with mail and news items, and their boats were destroyed. Four helpers in the Danish-Swedish Refugee Service, to which I belonged, were killed.

After the exodus of the Jews, I was kept busy with five or six fishing boats to carry saboteurs, politicians, deserters, and Allied airmen, together with the news. At this time we had our own arrangement on the Swedish side. And the Danes in Sweden would meet us halfway at the territorial borders, so that our boats did not have to enter into the Swedish ports unless we lost a message. . . . It wasn't easy in bad weather and dark nights to find one another. Sometimes our fishing boats were kept so busy with our underground export-import that they often didn't have time to fish. But [we would] buy a catch from the Swedish fishermen in order to come back with a little fish in [the Danish boats'] hull. All this time I functioned as a police officer until the day of September 19, 1944, at which time the Germans realized that they could not trust the Danish police to stop sabotage, and railroads [were] being blown to pieces by saboteurs.

Gestapo enforced with army and with German police troops surrounded all the Danish police stations and they arrested more than 2,000 officers from top to bottom. They were put on trucks and transported by a ship [inaudible], and thereafter, cattle cars in Germany to concentration camps in Buchenwald and Neuengamme, where many suffered sicknesses or died. Fortunately, I had left the station early in the morning. So when I returned, I found the station surrounded by Germans with small cannons and machine guns. And I saw my colleagues being pushed onto the trucks.

For more than forty years, I didn't talk much about resistance activities, except with coworkers. We thought that what we did was only a very small part of the big war. However, in 1985, Professors Samuel Oliner and Pearl Oliner researched a book called *The Altruistic Personality*. And their promotion of rescuers brought me and others invitations to tell our experiences at schools, colleges, universities, churches, and synagogues. I received many awards and an invitation . . . to visit Israel, where I was awarded at Yad Vashem. My best memories of all this [were] not the honor, or the heart-warming gratitude, but, just as well, to meet the other rescuers and hear their stories. I met Irene Opdyke from Poland who saved Jews in the basement of the home of a German high officer, whom she was forced to work for as a housekeeper. He found out one day and punished her severely. I met Tina Strobos [inaudible] from Holland, who, like in Anne Frank's story, kept Jews for months and months in a small apartment. [She was] not only afraid of Gestapo, but of being reported by neighbors for money. I met rescuers from Belgium, France, Yugoslavia, Bulgaria. And Ambassador Per Anger from Sweden, who, together with Raoul Wallenberg, saved thousands in Budapest, Hungary, by making out Swedish passports to thousands. I also met Mrs. [Yukiko] Sugihara who helped her Japanese husband [diplomat Chiune Sempo Sugihara] make passports from their embassy in Lithuania. And almost like in *Schindler's List*, I had the pleasure of meeting Hermann Gräbe, a German who, as described in Doug Huneke's book, *The Moses of Rovno*, saved many Jews from Germany as a German train master, taking the Jewish workers all the way from Ukraine into the Allied zone under great danger. Gräbe was one of the few Germans to witness against the Nazis at the Nuremberg Trial.

More than eleven thousand righteous rescuers have been recognized by Yad Vashem. The Jewish Foundation for [the Righteous] are active in finding and honoring rescuers. Also, they're able to support some with a small monthly stipend if they find them and some of them live in poor economic circumstances. Many, many rescuers never stepped forward and now [are] unknown, as they felt that what they did was no more than any good person should do for another in need.

Unfortunately, for mankind, many others during the Holocaust did not . . . concern themselves with the inhumanities right in front of their noses. Nobel Prize–winner Elie Wiesel said, "Let us remember that what hurt the victims the most is not the cruelty of the oppressor, but the silence of the bystander." Even today we are all bystanders to many discriminations. . . . Often I have been asked, [if] I can define what it takes to become an altruist and a rescuer? My parents taught me about compassion and conscience. . . . Maybe this learning prompted me to promote a motto and an action of what I call the three C's: "Compassion, conscience, consideration." The world would be a lovely place if we would all remember the value, the thee C's: compassion, conscience, consideration.

LAUREEN NUSSBAUM (b. 1927)

Were it not for Hans Calmeyer, Laureen Nussbaum may have been forced into hiding and potentially deported to a concentration camp like her childhood friends, Margot and Anne Frank. At first glance, Calmeyer— a German lawyer, member of the Wehrmacht (German army), and high-ranking official in the occupying government—seems an unlikely candidate for saving Jews in the Netherlands. In fact, Calmeyer's office was responsible for adjudicating "doubtful cases" of people registered as Jews in the Netherlands, who contested that registration, as they sought to avoid deportation. He leveraged this position to approve petitions that re-classified individuals as non-Jewish or half-Jewish, thus saving their lives, while trying to avoid arousing the suspicions of his superiors. Although being a "desk savior" was not as dramatic as the night-time smuggling efforts to ship Danish Jews to safety, Calmeyer's work was vitally important and effective. According to careful research conducted by Laureen Nussbaum, Calmeyer's bureaucratic approval of these petitions spared 3,700 Jews from deportation to Nazi camps. As a young law student, Calmeyer presciently declared, "There are ridiculously small things that are possibly bigger than the great heroic deeds. They do not inspire awe. On the contrary, they appear pitiful and foolish. And yet they are informed by more intrinsic, intimate value." Yad Vashem recognized Calmeyer as one of the "Righteous Among the Nations" in 1992. Laureen Nussbaum chronicles Calmeyer's life and its intersection with her own in the 2019 book, Shedding our Stars: The Story of Hans Calmeyer and How He Saved Thousands of Families Like Mine. *In Laureen's 2014 speech at Oregon State University, she describes how Calmeyer saved her family, and also discusses the general Dutch population and their resistance to the Nazis.*

... Well, I did not know, nor did my parents know that the Franks were in hiding in Amsterdam. [The Franks] had sort of concocted the story— and we became awfully good at concocting stories—that they had fled to Switzerland, which was not very probable, but possible. And to have it be possible was good enough for all of us to want to believe it. Mr. Frank had served as an officer in the German army in World War I. It was quite possible that he had some friends, non-Jews, who helped him. And so we hoped for the best and that was it, and we didn't give the Franks another thought, because we were surrounded by people who had to either allow themselves to be deported or had to try to go into hiding.

[T]he Frank family went into hiding the day after Margot got the call [to report for labor]. Margot was one of four thousand . . . young people ages sixteen to forty that got the call to report. The Franks did not report. My older sister also got a call to report for labor. Anne was too young; she was thirteen. I was too young; I was fifteen. But my sister . . . was older, and so she got a call.

But my family had done something which I alluded to earlier, when I said we were very good at making up tales. My mother, who had a non-Jewish mother, made up a story that she was not really sired by my Jewish grandfather, but that my grandmother had had some "hanky panky" with a non-Jewish man. It was all a big fat lie. But they [lied] very, very well. And because that case was pending, my sister got a deferment.

The way this game was played was that you got yourself a good Dutch lawyer. You wrote a petition in which you explained why you are claiming that you are not Jewish, or only half-Jewish, or only quarter-Jewish, or whatever your claim was. And that claim would go to an office in the Hague, the administrative capital of the Netherlands, and the headquarters of the German occupation. And there was a person by the name of Hans Calmeyer . . . who had to adjudicate cases where people claimed they were not as Jewish as their papers read. And so, at the point that my sister got a call, our petition had not been approved, and had not been disapproved either. It was pending, and that was enough at that moment to give my sister a deferment. And deferments were the name of the game. As long as you got a deferment, you were not deported just yet. . . .

So the story of my family went on the following way. By January of 1943 . . . a petition that [stated] . . . my mother was not Jewish at all—which was a big fat lie—was approved. And not accidentally approved . . . because the man [Hans Calmeyer], a German official who was in charge of adjudicating these cases, really was not a Nazi. He was not a member of the Nazi party. He was a German, of course, but he was not a Nazi. And he used his office to give his stamp of approval to as many people as he could. And as best as we know, he gave the stamp of approval in more than three thousand cases. And I take my family as an example. Other families were different. But in the case of my mother, the fact that her status was approved meant that the five of us—my two sisters and I . . . my father, who was now in a "mixed marriage"—we were all saved. So this man [Hans Calmeyer] definitely saved more people than the famous [Oskar] Schindler. And few, far too few, people know about him. But he was really a hero. Because to do this . . . while pretending to be a faithful servant of Hitler and go behind everybody's back to try to save as many people as you can, that's quite heroic really. . . .

Portrait of Hans Calmeyer in 1940. Courtesy of Filmkontor, Dr. Joachim Castan, Osnabrück.

Hans Calmeyer was part of the occupying German army when the Germans overran the Netherlands. He was in an air force communications unit. But as soon as the country was overrun, he was bored stiff and a lawyer friend of his—[Calmeyer] was a lawyer—found this job for him at the headquarters of the [German occupying government in the Hague]. And he readily took it, knowing that it would give him a possibility to do some good, and that's what he did. . . .

[*Question: "How do we know Hans Calmeyer had altruistic motives? . . . How do we know that he was really trying to help people?"*]

We know [that Calmeyer was acting in order to help others], number one, because of the number of cases that he approved of. And, for instance, in the case of my family, he never asked any questions that could have revealed the opposite. In other words, he didn't probe. He should have, according to the German authorities. But if a request, a petition, looked halfway plausible, he gave his stamp of approval. That was good enough. He did not [approve all of the petitions], because it would have been too obvious if he had approved them all. I mean, that would have been the end of his job, obviously. . . . He did as much as he could, but a few people [he] said "no" [to] because the petition was not plausible enough, and it was too transparent that it was fake. And he just said, "No." But he tried very hard.

[Question: "Did any of the people in Amsterdam protest in small ways, big ways? Did they know what was happening?"]

They [non-Jewish people in Amsterdam] knew what was happening, and they showed their sympathy, but protest, of course, in an occupied country is a very, very dangerous thing because you are the enemy of your occupiers, and the consequences are harsh. So, protest . . . was a lot to ask. But we did have a wonderful protest in Amsterdam in February of 1941, when the first Jews were arrested. There was a general strike and that was a fantastic gesture, but it was broken by force after two days. And so, there was no next strike . . . but it was a great gesture really.

. . . [T]here were many helpful people, and there were lots of good political jokes that we whispered to each other to show our disapproval. I mean, the bulk of the Dutch population was definitely anti-Nazi, which was of course also anti-occupation. It was much harder to be anti-Nazi in Germany than it was in Holland or Belgium, or France, where the Nazis were also the occupiers. But the overriding sentiment was "anti." At the time when the Nazis were victorious, they had 5 percent of the Dutch population with them. So that was all. But still . . . you have to watch out. Every twentieth person is a Nazi [in the occupied Netherlands]. I don't know which one, so you have to be careful, right?

[Question: During the Holocaust there were so many people who stood by and did nothing when they could have. Do you blame them in any little way?]

Do I blame the Dutch population for not rising up in the [*inaudible*]? It sounds like I should. I feel in a way I should, yes. But having lived through it, you know . . . it all comes bit by bit, in little steps. And every time there was a new decree, we would say, "Well, if that's all, we will live . . . make the best of it." And so it sort of creeps, sneaks up on you very gradually. And before you know, something terrible happens, but by small increments. And that's very devastating really. That's why people have to watch—watch out all the time—because sometimes the little things are just the beginning of big things.

EVA AIGNER (b. 1937)

We return here to Eva Aigner's testimony. As we learned in Chapter 1, Eva, her mother, and older sister, Ibolya, were forcibly relocated to the Budapest ghetto in 1944. In the following speech excerpt, Eva recounts how her mother managed to escape deportation and save Eva and Ibolya from execution on the banks of the Danube.

CONTENT WARNING: Mass murder, murder of children

As we were in the ghetto, one day the Hungarian Nazi officers marched in. And they started to gather the able-bodied people in the ghetto. My mother was thirty-eight years old at that time, and she was also picked out to be taken.

You can imagine how devastated my sister [Ibolya] and I were, two children. I was seven years old by that time, and she was fifteen. And our father was taken away [Eva's father had been taken to a forced labor camp in early 1943] and now they are picking our mother up. We didn't know how we were going to survive. And she was taken by these Nazi guards [at] gunpoint. We didn't know where. As we found out later, my mother was taken to a gathering place where they were loading these Jewish people onto wagons, and they were taken toward the concentration camp.

My mother couldn't live with the thought that she left her two little children behind. And the first time they opened the train car, she jumped [out] and started to run, started to escape. As she was running, a German soldier—mind you . . . a [member of the] Wehrmacht—yelled at her. [At] gunpoint, they said "Halt! Stop!" My mother speaks German. She spoke several languages. And she got down on her knees and grabbed this soldier's boots and says, "Please let me go. I have two little children. My husband is already taken. I don't know where he is. If I don't get back to my children, they'll never survive."

This man was a righteous man. He broke down. He pulled out the picture from his wallet and showed it to my mother, and he says, "Look, I have a wife and two children back there. I don't want to fight this war. But the only thing I can do for you . . . I'm going to turn away. If you can run, try to escape."

And my mother ran into the woods. And she walked back [to the ghetto]. It took several days to reach Budapest. She tore off her yellow star so nobody would recognize that she's a Jew. And she walked back into the ghetto where she last left us. [She] found out that that part of the ghetto was emptied just earlier that day. And she finds out [the

Arrow Cross] took around eight hundred people down to the riverfront of the Danube.[4] She ran down as fast as she could to the riverfront. . . . [I]t can only be a miracle that saved us. She recognized my sister's crying voice in the line. The eight hundred people who were standing at the riverfront were shot into the river. At that time they called the Danube, not the "blue Danube," but the "red Danube" because it was red from blood.

She bribed one of the guards and says, "Please! Let these children go!"

And he says, "Well, Jewish children cannot wander around in the city. I have to escort them back to the ghetto." So we were escorted back to the ghetto from the line and into the ghetto where my mother, my sister, and I survived. My father never came back. Neither did a lot of the rest of my family. They were killed, part of them in Czechoslovakia, part of them in Hungary. Just a very few of us were left.

ALTER WIENER (1926–2018)

Alter Wiener did not start speaking about his experiences of the Holocaust until 2000, the year he moved to Oregon. Encouraged by a fellow survivor to join the Oregon Holocaust Resource Center's Speakers Bureau, Wiener quickly became a tireless speaker and advocate for justice and Holocaust education, publishing a memoir in 2007.[5] Up until his death in December 2018, Alter spoke to over 1,000 audiences in Oregon and Southern Washington. Alter was thirteen years old when the Germans invaded his hometown in Chrzanów, Poland, and murdered his father. Two years later, Nazi agents sent him through five different camps where he was forced to perform hard labor. In the speech excerpt below, from his 2001 visit to Oregon State University, Alter describes the unexpected assistance he received at Gross Masselwitz, the third camp at which he was interned, and reflects upon his attitude toward Germans. We will hear more from Alter in the following chapter, including his views on Holocaust education and forgiveness.

Now in Gross Masselwitz it was a little bit easier in the respect that we didn't have to walk so many miles. We were in the same vicinity. And it was quite interesting, the kind of work we did. The Germans, as we all know, are very efficient. And everything was picked up at the front line, like [the weapons] of dead soldiers . . . or any equipment, any personal belongings. It [all] came to Gross Masselwitz. Our duty was to sort it, to clean it. And then to reship it.

[N]ow there is one episode in Gross Masselwitz that I would like to mention. It gave me a lesson in life about tolerance, and maybe you can learn from it, too. At one point, the Germans decided to convert a textile factory into an ammunition factory. And for that purpose, they asked us to dismantle a part of this factory right at the same time that in the other part of the factory German women, who had worked there for generations, continued to operate their [textile] machines. But there were signs all over telling those German women, "Don't look at the prisoners." "Don't have any contact with them." Because if you do, you risk your own life. You are doomed.

Now, one day, while I was dismantling a machine, a woman passed by after she had gone to the restroom. And she pointed to me. She hinted to a certain spot. I didn't know initially what she meant by that. But, out of curiosity, I went to that place, to that spot, and I saw under the crate a sandwich. Now, you have to remember, she risked her own life. A complete stranger. And she . . . repeated that noble act for thirty days, as long as I worked over there.

After the war, I went to that locality. I was prompted to reward her. I wanted so much to pay my debt because she really endangered her life for me, for a complete stranger. And, obviously, I didn't know her name. I could hardly remember her face. But nothing kept me back. I felt that that I owed something to that woman. Unfortunately, if you don't know the name, if you don't know the address—how can you locate somebody?

But that is the way I brought up my children. I always used to tell them, "I cannot make any generalization about any group."

[When] somebody asks me, "How come you don't hate all the Germans?" I always tell them, "How can I hate all the Germans [when] here was one of them that endangered her life for me?" And I'll never forget that woman. For years, it was my dream that I would be able to locate her.

JACK TERRY (1930–2022)

Jack Terry's life was saved several times by his fellow prisoners at the German labor camp, Flossenbürg. As Jack explains in the following speech excerpt, he avoided death by exhaustion and forced evacuation on a "death march" due to the sympathy and quick thinking of

non-Jewish prisoners, namely Milos Kucera and Carl Schrade. Arrested
by the Germans in 1942, Milos Kucera was Czech national who served as
camp clerk of Flossenbürg. Carl Schrade, a Swiss national and diamond
trader, was arrested in Berlin in 1934 and detained without any trial
for expressing anti-Nazi views. Schrade would spend a total of eleven
years imprisoned in German camps and served as a "Kapo"—a job that
required him to supervise other prisoners—at Flossenbürg. Both Kucera
and Schrade were privileged prisoners, and, as Terry explains, they used
their positions to help others when possible.[6] When he was liberated in
April 1945, fifteen-year-old Jack was the youngest surviving prisoner,
and likely the only Jewish prisoner who remained, at Flossenbürg.

My first work assignment was the [Flossenbürg] quarry where I had
to throw cubes of granite onto a little wagon. . . . After a day or two, I
had no skin on my fingers left. And after about two weeks, I felt that
now I understood what the words "Vernichtung durch Arbeit" mean—
which . . . translates [to] "extermination through work"—because I
couldn't last any longer.

Somehow, I managed to tell someone, most likely a man by the
name of Milos Kucera . . . a Czech inmate who was the record keeper in
the administration in the camp. [He testified] at the [war crimes] trials,
showing the [camp] records to the judges and the defenders and the
prosecutors. . . . I told him that I had experience working at the Heinkel
aircraft in Budzyń, and he arranged somehow, to transfer me to the
Messerschmidt factory. . . . And I worked there on the Messerschmidt
fighter planes. . . .

In February of 1945 . . . Kucera was able to get me a job in the laundry
and, well, it was a job in the interior. And there were two Hungarians
working there with me. One of them was [Ferenc Keresztes-Fischer] the
Interior Minister of Hungary. . . . They had special privileges; therefore,
they didn't eat the soup. It wasn't worth eating. But they still gave it to me.
I was able to use it, so I felt even able to help some of my friends—[fellow]
inmates—with some of it. And, also, occasionally I had to deliver sheets
to the bordello, which was a special barrack. . . . And there was a woman
who sometimes would sneak me a piece of bread. And it so happens that
in 1995—the 50th anniversary of the liberation of the camp—the same
woman recognized me, and we reminisced about it.

On April 15, [1945], I saw Milos Kucera again on the *Appellplatz* [roll call area]. And he said to me, "When the curfew whistle blows at nine o'clock, don't go to your barrack. But instead go to the laundry and go down from the boiler room. And there is a German prisoner, and he will take care of you."

The reason was that on the 16th, in the morning, all the Jews were to be evacuated on a "death march." So I was in the boiler room, in a tunnel. [It] went from the laundry to the kitchen, which was across the whole quadrangle from the *Appellplatz*. And I was lying on the heating pipes full of steam and hot water. And it was . . . unbearably hot. No food, no water. And I could hardly move. And in the morning I heard all kinds of commotion above on the ground, with firing and shooting. And, two days later, the Nazis temporarily disappeared because we could hear the artillery already from the US forces. . . . [T]here was a telegram sent from Heinrich Himmler to the commandants of Dachau and Flossenbürg ordering that no prisoners should fall into the hands of the Allies. And when I came out [of the tunnel], some of the Nazis had left. A Ukrainian fellow by the name of Nikolai saw me, and he says, "One Jew remains."

And so, lo and behold, the Nazis came back. And I . . . ran to Milos Kucera and I told him that, "I am again in danger."

So he sends me to the hospital, and he says, "See Carl Schrade." . . . He's an inmate. He was a Swiss national. [He testified] at the trial of the Flossenbürg camp. So I came there, and he changed my name to "Vaganov Vassily," gave me a Russian number with an "R" on it and told me that I was from Kharkov in the Ukraine. And then he put me in a typhus ward, where the Germans were less likely to go in because of the nature of the infectious process.

And in the evening, somebody—when they had called out my name for the piece of bread—somebody says to me, [in Russian] "Vassily, where are you from?" I said, "Kharkov." And he says to me [inaudible in Russian], "You are my Landsman [fellow countryman]." And . . . that was all the Russian I knew. So, I went to Carl, and I told him, and he put me in a different ward.

On the 20th of April, which also happened to have been Hitler's birthday, the whole camp was evacuated, except for all those in the hospital. 1,523 of us. . . . The first thing I did was sneak out of the hospital and go to the place where they had all the clothes and valuables. And I found civilian clothes and a rifle and ammunition. I figured, if [the Nazis] come back, at least, I'll die, but I may kill somebody. One of *them*. And instead, April 23rd, 10:50 in the morning, I saw a red-headed young man in an American uniform with a 90th Infantry Division patch. And I walk over to him, I give him the rifle, and he breaks [it] in two pieces. And that was the first day of liberation.

WALTER PLYWASKI (1929–2021)

Like Jack Terry, Walter Plywaski (featured in Chapter 1) also benefited from the assistance of fellow prisoners who had more privileges and resources at their disposal. In this brief excerpt from Walter's 2004 visit to Oregon State University, he describes falling ill in Dachau and shares his views about survival in the camps.

My brother [Bill] and I came on the "death march" from a small camp toward Dachau's main camp. Previously, we were in the Dachau main camp also, where I wound up in a so-called "clinic" because I had malnutrition holes in my legs. In the camps we called the disease "phlegmon." . . . [I]t's a malnutrition disease, and in Africa called "kwashiorkor." Your body simply starts making holes in your extremities in order to . . . pull proteins to build a cell for your liver or heart.

And so we were there [in the clinic in Dachau], and I got rescued by two Polish gentile "kapos." For whatever reason they decided to help me, I don't know. And they would show up at my bed with their hand over their number, so I wouldn't know it in case we were discovered. Five to six times a day they would bring me something to eat. A hard-boiled egg. I hadn't seen [one] in years. A slice of sausage, a slice of bread, a bit of butter. I started healing within two days. That's all it takes. And eventually, after about seven or eight days, they put a corpse in my bed and smuggled me out of there and I returned to my brother in the quarantine barracks.

You have to remember, in my opinion, any surviving Jewish person [who went] through this meat grinder, had to be helped by someone who was not Jewish. By a gentile, by a Christian, by an agnostic, but by a non-Jew. *Why?* We Jews were at the bottom of the sh** pile. We couldn't help each other. We couldn't help ourselves. And non-Jews had better treatment, had more food.

Notes

1 In late 1942 and 1943, nominally "neutral" Sweden offered asylum to Jews in Norway and Denmark. In addition, Swedish diplomatic officials in Budapest, among them Raoul Wallenberg, took the initiative to start issuing travel papers for Hungarian Jews in order to prevent their deportation in 1944. The impressive success of the Danish rescue effort causes one to wonder how many more Jewish lives could have been saved if other nations' governments and citizens had been more willing to take in Jewish refugees who stood in harm's way.

2 "Quisling" is a reference to Vidkun Quisling, a Norwegian fascist who collaborated with the Germans and took political power after the Norwegian government fled to London. His last name became a term used to describe a traitorous person who collaborated with occupying foreign forces.

3 Surprisingly, Duckwitz had been tipped off by leading Nazi official Werner Best, whom Himmler had ordered to oversee the deportations. Even though Best was a senior SS officer with no prior qualms about the "Final Solution," he believed that the deportation and murder of Danish Jews and communists would make his job— managing the German occupation in Denmark—more difficult since it would further upset the general Danish public who already resented German presence in their country.

4 During the winter of 1944–1945, Hungarian Arrow Cross fascists murdered thousands of Jews from the Budapest ghetto—including many children and the elderly—on the banks of the Danube River.

5 Alter Wiener, *64735: From a Name to a Number: A Holocaust Survivor's Autobiography* (Bloomington, IN: AuthorHouse, 2008).

6 Terry explained that, like Carl Schrade, Kucera "used his position to help others when he could." While in the army stationed in Europe in 1955, Terry drove to Zurich to thank Schrade for "saving his life." Alicia Nitecki and Jack Terry, *Jakub's World: A Boy's Story of Loss and Survival in the Holocaust* (Albany: State University of New York Press, 2005), 70.

5
Transitional Justice and Reconciliation

I felt that those of us who survived had some obliga-
tion to see that the things that happened to us weren't
repeated on other people, in other parts of the world.
—Thomas Buergenthal

In the immediate aftermath of a war that cost the lives of at least 60 million people, the Allied forces swiftly sprang to action to prosecute war criminals and forged new treaties and institutions that created the early foundations of international human rights law. In 1948, the United Nations—established to promote collective security and prevent another world war—officially recognized "genocide" as a grave international crime, and countries around the world pledged to prevent and punish genocide by ratifying the "Genocide Convention." Central to the effort to combat and condemn genocide were Holocaust survivors themselves, most notably Polish Jewish lawyer, Raphael Lemkin, who originated the term "genocide" in 1944 and advised the US legal team at the Nuremberg Trial. In addition to Lemkin, numerous survivors advanced postwar efforts to bring perpetrators to justice by providing witness testimony at trials and promoting peace and human dignity through educational efforts. In fact, the survivor speeches delivered at Oregon State University's Holocaust Memorial Week represent vital commemorative and educational work that advances the wide-ranging process of transitional justice, a concept of comprehensive social reckoning and healing that extends beyond individual perpetrators and those they victimized. Transitional justice entails a holistic effort to prevent the conditions that give rise to atrocities and inhumane actions in the first place. Many of the survivors featured in this chapter—and in this volume—remained silent about their painful experiences for decades, sometimes even refusing to speak about the subject with close family members. Yet they eventually chose to speak up in the hopes that by sharing their experiences, they could help combat—through empathy and education—the forces of hate, racism, and discrimination in order to prevent suffering in the future. In this closing chapter, the speakers weigh in how Germany has confronted the Holocaust and address the topic of historical reckoning and economic reparations—two key aspects of transitional justice. They also share their views on forgiveness and give advice to younger generations about confronting injustice.

LESLIE "LES" (1929–2021) AND EVA AIGNER (b. 1937)

For Eva and Leslie Aigner, thriving in Oregon represented a victory over the Nazis. As Leslie explained in the couple's 1998 visit to Oregon State University, "We started a new family, a new life. Defeating Hitler." Yet reckoning with their traumatic experiences took decades. The Aigners felt reluctant to share their stories with others until the 1990s. In the speech excerpt below, Eva and Leslie describe their path to involvement in commemorative and educational events for younger generations.

EVA AIGNER: [W]e didn't talk about the Holocaust for many, many, many years. It's painful. We didn't want to bring up these painful memories. We sort of buried it behind us. And we tried to live a life. We wanted to build a life and think about living, and not about dying. But then in 1992 the Anne Frank exhibit was going through Oregon. And about that time the Neo-Nazi movement was getting a hold.[1] My husband got very angry, and he said, "I have to speak up because this really happened. I lived it. How can people say, 'the Holocaust never happened'?" And we decided if you're not going to speak up and people [are] not going to meet

Eva and Leslie Aigner at their home in 2018. Photo by Sankar Raman. Courtesy of The Immigrant Story.

us—who lived the Holocaust—that [we would be] taking this with us one day to the grave.

. . .

LESLIE AIGNER: [A]s my wife mentioned, in 1992 when I retired, I heard all these stories that "this [the Holocaust] never happened." It made me mad enough to say that I will talk about it. So, since then, I have. I'm going to schools, colleges, churches—wherever I am invited—and talk[ing] about my experience. I'm not talking about the Holocaust philosophically. I don't bring too [many] numbers up because I'm just talking about my personal experience. All those [details] can be learned from a book. We're wanting survivors to find each other . . . even in this town, in Portland, we find each other.

In 1995, I was invited back to Landsberg [in Germany, where Leslie had been interned at a labor camp] . . . to commemorate the camps . . . by the mayor of Landsberg. And I met up with 114 survivors from those twenty-eight camps, who came from Israel [and] some from Europe, and about 80 of them from the United States. And we went to the camp sites . . . . And we went to Landsberg, and I met up with a gentleman who was on the very same train [to Dachau] I was on. He remembered the machine-gunning airplanes coming down [during an Allied air raid on German train cars]. And he escaped, but he went to the other direction.

What happened to him? Two German girls picked him up, hid him in a barn, and kept him, fed him. He told me the story. Personally, we didn't know each other. But we realized . . . that we were in the same place, at the same time. These German girls fed him and kept him hidden till the Allies liberated the area. This gentleman came to the United States and settled, became a successful businessman. And fifteen years later, he went back to Landsberg and wanted to look up these girls who saved him. He found them. And he was very appreciative, naturally. And one of the girls was married already, had a fifteen-year-old son. And the son became the mayor of Landsberg, who invited all the survivors who were available through the American Holocaust Museum [the USHMM]. The archives have our names. And whoever had been in those camps was invited.

Not many of us, not all of us went. . . . We didn't look forward to go[ing] back to the camps. We were very apprehensive going back, [about] how you will be [treated]. And . . . it turned out to be a good experience, a healing experience. Besides going to all these camp sites and commemorating and putting some flowers [at the sites] and [giving] talks in the area, . . . we had a town hall meeting. There was about 400 people in there—older people, high-schoolers, military people, all walks of life. The [Bavarian] governor was there. . . . I got to talk there. . . . I talked about a new time, after two generations, a new dialogue between the Germans and Jews. Some of the older [German] people were apprehensive. They remembered the camps, but they didn't want to talk about it naturally. But all in all, it was a very healing experience. . . .

EVA AIGNER: Some of the young people in this [town hall] meeting were accusing of the older German generation. Because for the first twenty-five years after the war, they didn't talk about the war. They didn't teach it in the schools, [did not teach about] the camps. These young people didn't know a thing about it. In fact, in this area in Landsberg, it was a young professor who discovered the old camp area and started to ask questions. So the young people were resenting it—that their parents and their grandparents didn't tell them what the history in their town was.

EVA MOZES KOR (1934–2019)

As we learned in Chapter 3, Eva Mozes Kor and her twin, Miriam, were inseparable and drew strength from each other during WWII and in the decades that followed. After Miriam's death in 1993, Eva Mozes Kor admits that she was "left with a lot of pain" and plagued by nightmares. Yet, as Eva describes in the 2016 speech below, she processed her grief— and her traumatic experiences as a child survivor of Nazi experimentation—in a radically unique way. Eva arranged to meet with a former Nazi doctor from Auschwitz, an encounter that would eventually culminate in Eva's decision to forgive the Nazis, even Dr. Josef Mengele, who had conducted inhumane experiments on Eva, Miriam, and nearly 3,000 other twins at Auschwitz. From that point forward, until her death in 2019, Eva was a tireless advocate for peace and forgiveness. She founded the CANDLES Holocaust Museum in Terre Haute, Indiana, penned three books about her experiences, and led yearly educational trips to Auschwitz. Eva's tremendous spirit and her journey are chronicled in a 2006 documentary, Forgiving Doctor Mengele.

CONTENT WARNING: Description of mass murder

I have forgiven the Nazis. I have forgiven everybody. I'm asked sometimes if you think we could change what happened. And, you know,
nobody can change what happened in the Holocaust, or any other tragedies. And even if all the Nazis would have been murdered—let's say
the all of the Nazis would have been caught and hanged—I still was an
eleven-year-old girl, an orphan. And I had a lot of medical problems. So
[killing all the Nazis would not] change my world. If anybody would've
asked me . . . twenty-three years ago, if I was going to forgive the Nazis,
I would've told you, "Please find a really good psychiatrist because you
must be crazy." [*The audience at OSU laughs at Eva's joke.*] I was a very
good victim. *What does that mean?* I was very angry with the world, and
I hated everybody.

And nothing changed in my life until Miriam died [in 1993]. I came
from a real estate open house on a Sunday afternoon. There was a message on my answering machine from my brother-in-law telling me, "I'm
sorry to inform you, but your sister died."

I immediately picked up the phone, called Israel, and I told him, "I
have never ever buried any member of my family." I wanted to bury my
sister. I wanted to say goodbye to her. And I wanted to say goodbye to
my kidney she was taking with her. [*Audience laughs.*][2] But my brother-
in-law said he cannot wait for me because the funeral is in ten hours.
Israel is seven hours ahead. And I was just in Israel in January; it took ten
hours, a nonstop flight from Newark to Tel Aviv, Israel. So, there was no
way for me to get there.

I was left with a lot of pain. I would wake up many nights suffocating,
and then I couldn't fall back asleep. I could feel the way Miriam died. Her
lungs were filled with cancer. And twins, in some strange circumstances,
can experience what the other twin did. I knew that eventually I would
do something in her memory. That is my way of coping with pain always.
So, two years later I opened CANDLES Holocaust Museum in Terre
Haute, Indiana [in 1995]. And my nightmares disappeared.

One month after Miriam died, unrelated to her death, I received a
telephone call from a professor—Dr. John Michalczyk at Boston College—who told me that he had heard me speak at a medical conference
at Boston School of Medicine. And he wanted me to come and lecture

to some doctors. And he said, "By the way, when you come, it would be really, really nice if you could bring with you a Nazi doctor."

I blurted out immediately, "Where on earth do you think I could find one of those guys? They are not advertising in the Yellow Pages."

So he said to me, "Okay, Eva, you like to joke a lot. Think about it. Maybe you can come up with some kind of an idea." And I did.

The next day I remembered that the last project that Miriam and I worked on was a documentary film by German television about the "Mengele twins." And in that documentary that aired in March of 1992, there was a Nazi doctor [Hans Münch] from Auschwitz. He was a friend of Mengele's. So, I figured he might be still alive. I took a letter to Germany, to the television station, and asked them to give me Dr. Münch's telephone number in the memory of Miriam, because they refused to give it to me in 1992. I received the telephone number. We contacted Dr. Münch, and he said he was not willing to go to Boston, but he was willing to meet with me at his house in Germany.

Now, I was getting ready to go and meet a Nazi doctor. You have no idea how scared I was. What I remembered about Nazi doctors, I did not want to experience again. But I was curious what I might learn. And I was curious: Why was this Nazi doctor willing to meet with me? We arrived at his house. He treated me with the utmost respect, kindness, and consideration.. . . [W]e were sitting outside . . . on metal chairs. And this eighty-two-year-old guy went back to the house five times. Each time he came back with a pillow that he handed me.

After the fifth pillow, I said, "Excuse me, Dr. Münch. What are you doing?"

He said, "I want to make sure that you are comfortable sitting on those metal chairs."

A Nazi doctor being concerned about my comfort? It did not compute in my mind. But he gave me a good interview about what he did in the camp. And then out of the blue—I never planned to ask the question—I heard myself say . . . "Dr. Münch, while you were in Auschwitz, did you ever walk by the gas chamber? Did you ever go inside? Do you have any idea the way it works?"

And he immediately said, "This is my problem. This is my nightmare that I live with every single day of my life." And he went on describing the operation of the gas chamber. . . . Dr. Münch was stationed outside, looking through a peephole. When the people [in the gas chamber] . . . stopped moving, Doctor Münch knew that everybody was dead. And he signed one death certificate. No names [on it], just the number of people that were killed. . . .

And I asked him to come with me to Auschwitz in 1995 and sign a document [describing how the Nazis murdered Jews in the gas chambers][3] at the ruins of the gas chamber where it happened, in the company of six witnesses. And he immediately told me, "I would love to."

So, I got back to Terre Haute, Indiana, very, very excited that I will have a unique document signed by a Nazi. That was important to me. And I wanted to thank this Nazi doctor for his willingness to document the gas chamber. I did not know how to thank a Nazi doctor. I did not want to tell anybody but my friends and family because I knew they would try to convince me not to do it, and I didn't want anybody telling me not to do it. I didn't know how to find a gift for [Doctor Münch]. I went to the local Hallmark shop. I went to a section called "thank you cards." I began reading card after card after card, for two and a half hours.

Two ladies came up to me, "You have been reading those cards for a long time. Are you finding what you're looking for?"

Eva Mozes Kor (*at left in foreground*) with former Nazi doctor Hans Münch (*at right in foreground*) at Auschwitz in 1995. Courtesy of CANDLES Holocaust Museum and Education Center.

I said, "Not really."

"Well, what are you looking for? Maybe we can help you find it."

I said, "No, thank you very much." I left the card shop, but I could not give up my idea of finding a meaningful gift for Dr. Münch. . . .

For the next ten months while I was cooking, cleaning, doing the laundry, driving the car—when my mind wasn't too busy—I brainstormed by myself. Lot of ideas popped into my mind, until, ten months later, a simple idea. How about a letter of forgiveness from me to Dr. Münch? I immediately knew that he would like it.

But what I discovered for myself was life-changing, I discovered that I had the power to forgive. No one could give me that power, and no one could take it away. It was all mine to use it in any way I wish. And I want you to know that every single one of you here have the power to forgive. No one can give it to you. No one can take it away from you. It's yours to use it as you wish.

I began writing my letter. I didn't know how to thank a Nazi doctor or to write the letter. It took me four months. And then it occurred to me that somebody might read my letter, and my spelling in English is embarrassingly bad. And I didn't want to be embarrassed. So, I called my former English professor to correct my spelling. . . . We met three times, and the third time she said to me, "Now, Eva, you are forgiving this Dr. Münch. Your problem is not with Dr. Münch. Your problem is with Dr. Mengele." I tried to debate that. But she said to me, "Eva, I had been giving you a lot of favors, correcting your letter. Now I want you to do me a favor. When you go home tonight, pretend that you are talking to Josef Mengele and telling him that you forgive him because I want to see how you would react to it."

Well, it sounded like an interesting idea. I went home, closed the bathroom door, picked up a dictionary and made a list of a lot of nasty words. [*The audience laughs.*] I read the words out clear and loud. And at the end I said, "In spite of all that, I forgive you." I found it a very interesting feeling. Wow! This is my last interaction with Josef Mengele, and there is my forgiveness. He can never erase it. It will stand forever. I wasn't hurting anybody. So, I reasoned, why couldn't I forgive him? It made me feel good. And, if I forgave Mengele, I decided to forgive everybody who has ever hurt me.

So, this is the way we arrived in Auschwitz [in 1995]. Doctor Münch came with his daughter, son, and granddaughter. I took my son and my daughter. Doctor Münch signed his document. I read mine and signed it. And I immediately felt that all the pain I carried around for fifty years was lifted from my shoulders, that I was no longer a victim of Auschwitz, nor was I a prisoner of my tragic past. I was free of Auschwitz and I was free of Mengele.

. . .

"Forgiveness is the best revenge," because the moment you forgive the perpetrator, they no longer have any hold or power over your life. Forgiveness creates a feeling of wholeness in thought, spirit, and action, going in the same direction, creating a force for good. It's free. Everybody can afford it. And if you do not like the way you feel as a free person, you can always go and take your pain back. Nobody will stop you. . . . [I]f any of you have any problems that you have difficulty coping with, all you need is a piece of paper and a pen. Write a letter to the person or people who have hurt you. Do not mail them the letter, or give it to them, because that relationship is poison. The forgiveness letter is for you. . . . And if you feel . . . liberated, pass it on to other people. Because I need everybody's help to sow those seeds of peace throughout the world.

THOMAS BUERGENTHAL (1934–2023)

A child survivor of Auschwitz, Thomas Buergenthal came to the US in 1951 with only two years of schooling, but he became an esteemed international human rights lawyer, professor of law, and a judge for the International Court of Justice. Thomas was born in Czechoslovakia in 1934, where his German Jewish parents settled shortly after the Nazis took power. Four years later, following the November pogroms, the family fled to Poland and—after a failed attempt to escape to England—eventually ended up in Kielce ghetto. While in Poland, Thomas's mother visited a fortune-teller, who proclaimed Thomas a "lucky child." Such a label might seem ironic considering that Thomas was deported to Auschwitz and separated from his family, yet he managed to elude the "selections" at Auschwitz and—at ten years of age—was one of only three children who survived the "death march" to Sachsenhausen. After the war ended, Thomas was placed in an orphanage, but his mother located him two years after their separation at Auschwitz. He writes about his experiences and his reunion with his mother in his memoir, A Lucky Child: A Memoir of Surviving Auschwitz as a Young Boy. *Thomas Buergenthal visited Oregon State University on the seventieth anniversary of the liberation of Sachsenhausen (by the Soviets) to discuss the legacies of the international human rights treaties, laws, and courts established in the shadow of World War II and the Holocaust. In the excerpt below, he shares his optimism about international human rights progress and discusses what younger generations can do to prevent genocide and other human rights abuses.*

Thomas Buergenthal at Oregon State University in 2015. Courtesy of the Oregon State University Special Collections and Archives Research Center, Corvallis, Oregon.

I'm an international lawyer. I am a Holocaust survivor, just on the side. [*Audience laughs, and Thomas smiles.*] But my experience really is in international law, and I specialized . . . in international human rights. I felt that those of us who survived had some obligation to see that the things that happened to us weren't repeated on other people, in other parts of the world. And I wanted to see how one could do this. I still don't know how you do it. But . . . we should have a commitment to try to prevent these things from happening. And that is really what I've spent my professional life doing. . . .

[W]hen I first started in the . . . international human rights field, nobody was very much interested in it. And I should also tell you that when I came to the United States, nobody was interested in hearing anything about the Holocaust. You'll be surprised to hear, it was not only non-Jews, but Jews weren't interested in it either. This [interest in the Holocaust] came much later. Which surprised me when I came to this country. The Germans where I went to school were very preoccupied with [the war and the Holocaust]. They didn't dare ask questions; they wanted to. Here, they just [*Thomas pauses.*] . . . there was total silence. and I've still never understood it. . . .

. . .

There are many skeptics, I'm sure. When you hear there are international treaties for the protection of human rights, there are international courts, and . . . still, genocide is still being committed. [Skeptics] say, "What is it all worth?" Let me tell you, it's worth it. It takes time. I'm always struck by Americans [who] say, "How come they haven't done this or that? Why haven't they stopped this terrible activity in one country or the other?" Why haven't we? Why has it taken us so long to do away with racial discrimination in this country? It takes time. So let me just give you a little lesson on what I teach in my classes about the existing international institutions. . . . I think there's nothing worse than being skeptical about these things because it's just an excuse for doing nothing.

. . .

Basically we have today . . . for example in Europe, we have the European Convention of Human Rights. And we have a court that has existed since 1953. It's become basically the European Constitutional Court dealing with human rights matters. It's the first in the world. It has decided many, many cases, has held almost every government in Western and Eastern Europe responsible for some violations of human rights. Including many governments who thought that they were the embodiment of human rights protection. Nevertheless, each government historically has something in their closet that they want to hide, and consequently, it has come out.

We now have an Inter-American Court on Human Rights, on which I served, which really was a court that was modeled on the European Court of Human Rights. The problems that we had in Latin America were much more complicated than the problems Western Europe had when that court was first established. But it's doing some fascinating work today with many more cases.

There is a new African Court, which has the biggest problems. It's not easy to have a human rights tribunal in Africa considering the problems they face—poverty, dictatorships, and everything else. But it exists.

The United Nations has adopted a large number of treaties, starting with the Genocide Convention [in 1948]. We now have also the first ever—after Nuremberg—International Criminal Court, established in 2002. We have waited since Nuremberg for this court to be established. It has finally been established . . . [and] has more than 130 member states. Unfortunately, not the United States, not Russia, not China, and a few other countries. We're [the United States] always holdouts, with some countries with which we really don't want to be identified. But here we are.

The United States incidentally never ratified the American Convention on Human Rights. So when I was elected to the court, I was the only American elected. And no American has ever been elected to that court again. Because the US couldn't nominate, Costa Rica wanted to nominate me. And they said, that's the last time an American will serve on that court until the United States ratifies that convention. . . . [W]e are still waiting.

There are two courts that have been extremely active—so-called "ad hoc" international criminal tribunals created after the Bosnian conflict, and another one created after Rwanda. These two ad hoc tribunals have tried quite a large number of people that are sitting now in jail. These were tribunals established that were supposed to last only two or three years. . . . And they are still operating because it's such a difficult task . . . every so often one more criminal is found.

Editor's note: The UN established the International Criminal Tribunal for the former Yugoslavia in 1993 and the International Criminal Tribunal for Rwanda in 1994. After twenty-three years of operation, the ICTs for the former Yugoslavia and Rwanda dissolved in 2016 and 2017, respectively.

But all the international criminal law we now have has been created by these courts and it's an impressive thing that is going on. Most Americans are totally unaware of the existence of these courts. . . .

[*Question: "What can we, as American college students, do to prevent genocide in the future?"*]

First of all . . . one of the most important things is to familiarize yourself with what is available to do. For example, there are a lot of non-governmental organizations [NGOs] in the United States, and also abroad, who work in those different fields and work in different countries.

Find out what they are doing, what they suggest should be done. But to me, also, the most important thing is for American students to find out more about the possibilities. For example, what treaties exist? That's not too complicated legally. And begin to see what [the treaties] do. What kind of access is provided for outsiders to have an impact?

And the other thing [to do] is to organize. More and more, non-governmental organizations arise from a group of students getting together and deciding to pick . . . one country, for example, publicize what's going on in that country, and work that way. There are many, many opportunities. But the best thing, for starters, I would just draw up a list of some of the American and international NGOs that work. All of you know Amnesty International.[4] But there are many, many others. Very good ones in the United States. "Americas Watch" [now called "Human Rights Watch"[5]] and other watch committees, for example. "Human Rights First"[6] [is] another American one. And see what they're doing and . . . what you could do working with them.

. . .

[*Question: "What advice can you give to college students to help them to become better people and to prevent things like this from happening again?"*]

First of all, I think what is so important is to study what's going on in the world. . . . You've got tremendous opportunities. And most of us never really take all of the opportunities. You have a great library [at Oregon State University], a lot of possibilities. The first thing to do with these four years that you have here is to familiarize yourself with the world. And, at that point, decide what you really think is important. . . . But the most important starting point is to learn more. . . . Find out what's going on in the world and then decide what you feel needs to be done. Don't get an old man to tell you what you need to do. [*Audience laughs.*] But really, you will be surprised what you find. There are so many opportunities to do important things that you would enjoy doing, if you just knew that they were available.

[*Question: Do you believe that the legal definition of genocide is appropriate? What is the difference between genocide and mass murder?*]

There's a differentiation in the Genocide Convention [1948 UN Convention on the Prevention and Punishment of the Crime of

Genocide]. . . . [For mass murder] to be [considered] genocide requires two intentions: One, the intent to commit a crime, and the specific intent to commit genocide, which is a crime involving ethnic, religious, or [racial] killings. But there are . . . a number of other crimes. Like, for example, crimes against humanity, which isn't genocide because it . . . is just a large-scale international criminal offense. And there is a general sort of assumption among international lawyers, and among the public at large, that the worst possible crime is genocide. I think we're exaggerating that. This is my personal view. I think a serious crime against humanity is every which [way] as bad as genocide. And one of the problems is, for example, that genocide is defined in many ways, but it does not define political opinion as a basis for your killing. And that is something that I think is missing. And it is missing because the Soviets tried to keep it out of the Genocide Convention [when the treaty and legal definition for genocide was being drafted]. So, to my mind—and I've been connected with the US Holocaust Museum for a long time as chairman of the committee that dealt with the subject—I always speak of "genocide and related crimes." So the related crimes to me, or crimes against humanity—massive crimes—are every which [way] to me as important as genocide itself. That doesn't mean that genocide isn't very, very important. But let's not forget the other killings. For example, what is happening today in North Korea is not genocide. It's a crime against humanity of the most unbelievable type, but it doesn't really qualify as genocide.

. . .

[*Question: With all of your experiences, how do you manage to be passionate, but not vengeful?*]

[W]hen I first came out of the camp and . . . I was reunited with my mother, we lived in a house with a balcony. And on weekends, German families, in the old German tradition, would walk into the forest, up to the hill past us. And I kept saying to my mother, "I wish I had a machine gun, to kill them like they killed my father and my grandparents." And then gradually, I began to think about it. And I had a friend [Odd Nansen] from the concentration camp. A Norwegian, who was there for different reasons. He published a book [*Day to Day: One Man's Experience in Nazi Concentration Camps*] in Germany, a diary of his experience in Sachsenhausen . . . that was partially dedicated to me, and published in

Norwegian, in English, and in German. And he gave all of the proceeds of his book to German refugees. And he'd spent three years in German camps. And I said to him, "Why would you do this? These are the guys who did this all to us."

We had a number of long discussions. And his basic point was that "hate begets hate." And we have to—if we want to stop these killings—we have to stop hating. And I thought about it and thought about it. And it has affected my total attitude . . . I don't hate Germany.

Incidentally, Germany today is a very different Germany. So that discussion has had a tremendous impact on my thinking about how you confront these activities. This man [Odd Nansen] incidentally had saved my life in Sachsenhausen [by sharing some of his bread rations]. So, to me, this was an eye-opener, and I wish many people who've had my experience, who have similar experiences in other genocides, have somebody who can talk to them the way I was talked to, and to stop the hatred. Because it doesn't do any good. It hurts us internally. It has terrible consequences.

ALTER WIENER (1926–2018)

Three months before Alter Wiener's death, he testified to the Oregon state legislature in September 2018, declaring, "At this time, we should all try incessantly to divert the rivers of hatred so that another Holocaust should never, never happen again. . . . Learning about the Holocaust is not just a chapter in recent history, but a derived lesson on how to be more tolerant, more loving, and that hatred is eventually self-destructive. Be better, rather than bitter."[7] Thanks to Alter's words and legacy, in 2019 Oregon became the eleventh state to legally require Holocaust and Genocide education in K-12 public schools. In the speech excerpt below from his 2001 visit to Oregon State University, Alter reflects on the topic of forgiveness and his hope for a better world.

I have just questions. I don't have the answers. Why did they take me? Why did they take me to a concentration camp? Why did they beat me? Why did they knock out my teeth? I have no answers. But I don't hate. I'm willing to forgive.

Lewis and Clark Law School Dean Robert Klonoff (far left) introduces Alter Wiener (far right) during a ceremony to award Wiener an honorary doctorate from Lewis & Clark College in 2009. Courtesy of the Oregon Jewish Museum and Center for Holocaust Education.

Somebody who really helped me [was Simon Wiesenthal, who wrote] a very interesting book called *The Sunflower*. . . . And it's his history when he was in a concentration camp. At one point . . . his job was to clean the hospital. In this hospital on one bed there was a German officer—a Nazi—dying. And he called to [Simon], told him, "Come here, I want . . . I want to make a confession to you. I killed so many innocent women and children and men. And I want to [inaudible]. I want to ask you to forgive me. I want to die in peace."

So, Simon Wiesenthal couldn't make up his mind. On one hand, he would be willing to forgive that officer. On the other hand, how could he? He had no right to talk on the behalf of all those people who are not here anymore. And, in that book [*The Sunflower*], Simon Wiesenthal asks fifty-three prominent people from all over the world—clergymen, philosophers of theology, politicians— "How would you have acted in my, in this kind of situation? Would you be willing to forgive?" And their answers are so different. No two people have the same answer. They all have difficulties coming to a decision. . . .

[W]hen I was liberated, I thought maybe there's going to be a better world. A better world order. I suffered so much. I paid such a high price.

Maybe there's going to be a better world? Unfortunately, many events have taken place since then, like in Bosnia, or Somalia, or the Middle East, or in Kosovo, and this is discouraging to a certain extent. Because I thought that when we were liberated, there was going to be no more suffering. No more tormentors. But unfortunately, there is. . . .

I remember a few years ago when I went to a [Holocaust] commemoration . . . in New York City. I came out and a TV crew approached me, and they asked me, "Are you a survivor?" I told them, "Yes." "So how do you relate to the events in Kosovo?" I told them, "I feel very bad about it . . . that there is still so much cruelty in this world." But there's a big difference. When I was in concentration camp, I felt completely abandoned by the world community. Here at least, today, somebody cares. Is it the United Nations? Is it the United States? Somebody cares. We felt completely abandoned. That was the worst part of it.

. . .

And I still . . . I don't hate German people as a whole, especially today's generation. It's not their fault what their ancestors did. And if I get my pension . . . for my labor [in Nazi-run camps], I'm getting $500 a month.[8] This doesn't bring my family back.

. . .

The reason why I'm here [at OSU] and the reason I lecture many places . . . [is that young people] don't know anything about it. And you have to enlighten them. Because there is a message. There is a silver lining and a message, in my experience. It would be very sad if somebody were to come to me and say, "The Holocaust didn't exist. It didn't happen." And there are . . . people who try to deny the Holocaust, which is very painful. And it's stupid too. Because the events of the Holocaust, of WWII, are so well documented. Thanks to photography and other technology, you go to museums and see pictures taken by the German soldiers while they were committing those criminal acts. It is evidence. How can anybody claim it didn't happen? That is the reason [I lecture to so many schools]. And children do appreciate [it]. I can tell you, I have three hundred letters at home from children and teachers, and they say that I made a difference in their life. First of all, they are going to appreciate more of what they have. They are not going to take anything for granted. And above everything else, they are going to be informed.

JACQUES BERGMAN (1923–2001)

Auschwitz survivor Jacques Bergman (see Chapter 2) admitted to the audience at Oregon State in 1999 that he "never told my brother what happened to me until recently." Like the Aigners, Jacques was hesitant to discuss his horrific experiences or come forward publicly as a survivor. Beginning in 1992, however, Jacques was compelled to share his story. In a brazenly honest question-and-answer session with the audience in Corvallis excerpted below, Jacques grapples with anger and indifference that he has experienced and encountered as a Holocaust survivor, and reveals his misgivings about whether justice has really been served.

[*Question: Have you ever gone back to Europe?*]

I have gone back to Holland several times. I've gone back to Vienna once because I wanted to find out what happened to my parents. . . . I know several survivors who go back to Auschwitz, and Bergen-Belsen, whatever, Mauthausen. You couldn't pay me to go back [to the camps]. You couldn't pay me.

[*Question: How often do you think about what happened to you?*]

Almost every day. It never left me. There is always a newspaper article, a TV show, a movie—doesn't matter what—you're reminded of [what happened]. And everything comes back again. I haven't spoken about this for forty years. And a few years ago . . . there was an exhibit in Portland, the Anne Frank exhibit. And I was asked to speak about my experience. I was a little bit reluctant. And at the same time, a guy from England by the name of [David] Irving, a Holocaust denier, came to Portland and spoke to a group of Nazis there. And I got mad. So I told whoever was in charge of the exhibit, "Sign me up!" And from that moment on, I spoke. I speak to eighth graders, to high schools . . . and colleges, whatever.

[*Question: After what happened to you, how did you adjust to life in the US after the war?*]

I tried to put it out of my mind completely. But I wasn't very successful. Like I say, not the first . . . forty years. . . . The reason I didn't talk about [the Holocaust was] because nobody wanted to hear about it. You know, people came back from the war. They were busy with their own lives. They didn't want to listen to horror stories. They didn't want to listen to the Holocaust. They weren't—most of the people—weren't even aware of it. So I kept quiet. So I tried to keep it out of my mind and tried to make a start from the beginning. Tried to make a living. Tried to do something with my life.

[*Question: Were you angry at the American people?*]

Uh, I'm angry now. I wasn't angry then. But I'm . . . sometimes I'm angry now because America did very little, very little. It's coming out now. But they didn't do anything about the solution. Look at the ship, the *Saint Louis* was sent back to England.[9] You had to have affidavits[10] in order to get to the United States. . . .

. . .

[*A not fully audible question is raised from audience member about post-war justice and reparations for Holocaust survivors.*]

[S]ome of them [countries like Germany and corporations that utilized "slave labor" during the war] are paying back now, I understand. Um, I don't know about justice. Come on. You know, the funny part—well, it's not funny—but the factories paid the Germans, paid the Nazis, for each laborer between 4 and 5 marks a day. They paid them for it. They paid for everything, even the people who got transported, deported. They had to pay. The railroad made up tickets. They had to pay for that, on paper. So, everybody worked for the Nazis. Everybody. The farmer who grew those rotten potatoes. The railroads. The people who built the ovens. They're making beer now.[11] Same people. Everybody got paid.

MARION BLUMENTHAL LAZAN (b. 1934)

Marion Blumenthal Lazan (featured in Chapters 1 and 3) returned to Germany for the first time in 1995, on the fiftieth anniversary of her family's liberation, in order to visit Bergen-Belsen and the grave of her father, who passed away from typhus shortly after liberation. In the years that followed, Marion, her husband Nathaniel, and their children have made many return trips for educational and commemorative purposes. In the speech excerpt below, Marion discusses how the German government and her hometown of Hoya have reckoned with the terrible crimes and persecution committed against Jews during the 1930s and 1940s.

[After visiting Bergen-Belsen in 1995] we also went to our former hometown of Hoya, near Hannover. And there we were greeted by public officials who apologized over and over again. Then there was a young non-Jewish couple, born after the war, and they took us to the Jewish cemetery, which was in terrible disarray. [It] had not been cared for since 1938. [They] took us to our family plot and there, among the toppled-over stones, was a brand-new shiny granite foot stone with the inscription [in German], "In memory of the desecrated plot of the Blumenthal family. Hoya, 1894 to 1938." [It had been] placed there by this non-Jewish young couple, unbeknownst to us. A most beautiful, generous, kind gesture. I never thought that I would refer to non-Jewish Germans in such glowing terms. And it's people like these that renew one's faith in humanity. And they've become wonderful, wonderful, dear, dear friends of ours.

And each time we return [to Germany], I speak in schools, universities . . . sometimes in churches. And [my speeches are] tremendously well received, but also difficult for today's young people to hear. After all, their grandparents' and great-grandparents' generation were responsible for such terror.

Then we returned in 2010 because a brand new public high school in my former hometown was named in my honor. So now we have the "Marion Blumenthal Oberschule" of Hoya. [There was] a tremendous celebration. And [it was] very courageous for this little town to redress what happened so many years ago, in their midst. And the night . . . the celebration of naming the school, we commemorated the "Night of Broken Glass" on the site where our synagogue once stood. Difficult trips, yes, but no regrets having returned.

Germany is doing an outstanding job in continually reminding their people as to what has happened. It is mandatory for the subject [the Holocaust] to be taught in their schools. And they have various ways of reminding their people. We had the opportunity to see the parliament in Berlin. There were . . . walls and walls of murals depicting the "Night of Broken Glass."

And they have the *"Stolpersteine"* . . . it's a "stumbling block." You don't really stumble over. It is a metal plaque deeply embedded in the sidewalk in front of the home, where a [Jewish] person once lived and never returned. With a name, date of birth, date of [death], and where, how . . . he or she died. I mean, it's enormous history on that little plaque. And you can't help but see it. So there are various ways of the population is Germany reminding its people. And that has to be commended, for sure.

[*Question: Do you think that younger Germans . . . are open looking at their grandparents' and great grandparents' role in German history?*]

They have a very, very difficult time. I remember speaking at a middle school in Germany, just going back a number of years. And there was one young lady [who] burst out crying. She had asked her grandparents . . . what they thought of the Second World War. Where were they? What did they do during that time? And they would not answer. They changed the subject. And that made [the young lady] think that perhaps [her grandparents] had something negative to do with what happened back then. It's very, very difficult for this generation, today's generation to hear all this. But they do want to hear it. And they see that I'm not an angry person. . . . They don't shy away from wanting to hear about it. So, it's important. . . . It's sad, but that's how it is.

Notes

1 On October 16, 1992, infamous Holocaust denier David Irving gave a sparsely attended talk at Mt. Hood Community College's Visual Arts Center at the invitation of a group that called itself "The Siegfried Society." According to *The Oregonian*, the number of anti-Irving protestors outnumbered the event's attendees by a three-to-one ratio. Irving's visit occurred one week after the month-long "Anne Frank and the World" exhibit opened to the public at the First United Methodist Church in downtown Portland. Ashbel S. Green and John Snell, "Just Handful Hear Irving's Hoax Theory," *The Oregonian*, October 17, 1992.

2 Eva donated a kidney to Miriam in 1987.

3 Dr. Münch's signed document can be viewed at https://candlesholocaustmuseum.org/educational-resources/dr-hans-munch.html.

4 https://www.amnesty.org/.

5 https://www.hrw.org/.

6 https://humanrightsfirst.org/.

7 The speech was published on YouTube by the Oregon Jewish Museum and Center for Holocaust Education. https://www.youtube.com/watch?v=o8PAka_tTWk.

8 This is a reference to a pension paid by the German government as a form of restitution. Since 1951, the Conference on Jewish Material Claims Against Germany (Claims Conference) has secured material compensation for Holocaust survivors around the world. For more information, visit https://www.claimscon.org.

9 The *St. Louis* was a luxury cruise liner that traveled between Hamburg, Germany, and Havana, Cuba. In May 1939, the ship left Hamburg with over 900 passengers, most of whom were Jewish refugees of Nazi persecution. When the ship arrived in Havana, the Cuban government allowed only 28 passengers to disembark and denied entry to the rest of the passengers. (Apparently, a large number of Cuban visas had been sold illegally by the director-general of immigration, who had embezzled a small fortune from the sale.) The ship's captain made numerous calls to city officials along the eastern seaboard, but officials in the United States and

Canada refused to permit entrance of the ship or its refugee passengers. President Roosevelt and the State department did not pursue special measures to permit refugees. Many passengers aboard the *St. Louis* frantically cabled the White House and US government to plead for asylum. Receiving no help from US or Canadian officials, the *St. Louis* sailed back to Europe, which stood three months away from the outbreak of WWII. Thanks to negotiations carried out by Jewish aid organizations, none of the passengers were sent back to Germany; most were granted permission to enter Britain, Belgium, France, and the Netherlands. But by the fall of 1939, 532 passengers of the *St. Louis* would find themselves again trapped during Nazi invasions into Western Europe, around half of them (254 in all) perished during the Holocaust. "Voyage of the *St. Louis*," *USHMM Holocaust Encyclopedia*, https://encyclopedia.ushmm.org/content/en/article/voyage-of-the-st-louis.

10 During the 1930s and 1940s, a person seeking to immigrate to the United States needed to be sponsored by two current US citizens or permanent residents. According to the US State Department, an "Affidavit of Support" is a "document an individual signs to accept financial responsibility for the applicant who is coming to live in the United States." You can learn more about immigration requirements during the WWII-era here: "Documents Required to Obtain a Visa," USHMM Holocaust Encyclopedia https://encyclopedia.ushmm.org/content/en/article/documents-required-to-obtain-a-visa.

11 This is likely a reference to Topf & Sons company.

Afterword

The Evolution of Holocaust Memorial Week at Oregon State University: An Interview with Paul Kopperman

Abridged and edited interview of Paul Kopperman, Professor Emeritus of History and Former Chair of Oregon State University's Holocaust Memorial Week Committee, conducted by OSU History Masters students Rebecca Murray and Daniel Arellano in February 2023.

How did you become involved with the Holocaust Memorial Week? How would you describe the first few years of the program?

The Holocaust Memorial Committee dates from 1987. It was a product initially of the Office of Academic Affairs, [within] the Provost's Office at Oregon State University. At that time Graham Spanier was the provost and his chief assistant was an Academic Vice-President, Miriam, or, as everybody knew her, "Mimi" Orzech. The 1980s had been somewhat difficult for the local Jewish community. There had been a great deal of antisemitic activity: hate mailings, et cetera. Very, very nasty stuff, and continual across particularly the period from 1983 to 1986. And that was certainly fresh in the memories of many of us. On the other hand, it had also been a period for us to become more aware of just what would be available to us if we were going to try something to counter this. And there was a grand consensus that the more people knew about the Holocaust, then the less antisemitism—particularly extreme antisemitism—would be manifest.

Holocaust education of one sort or another was accepted by many of us [on the committee] as being important, as being a key to—this was certainly not its only purpose, but among other things—reducing the prevalence of antisemitism in American society and the number of antisemitic incidents in any given year. . . . [T]his was a time when The Holocaust Memorial Museum in Washington, DC, was not yet opened. However, there was a board already active at the museum. Among other things, they were anxious to try to get universities, colleges, municipalities, to do something to observe a weekly program that had been initiated by Congress in the late 1970s, the same time that they authorized the construction of the Holocaust Memorial Museum in DC. This board was responsible for encouraging us [at OSU] to do something to observe what was usually called "Holocaust Remembrance Week," which had likewise been established by Congress in the late '70s.

Up to this time any sort of recognition of the Holocaust in the schools or on university campuses was quite limited. When I went to college, there were extremely few courses taught on the Holocaust. And I know because I looked for them. I really wanted to take a course on the subject and couldn't find one.

The Holocaust board [the *US Holocaust Memorial Council*] started sending out posters and ideas for remembering the Holocaust: things that would be used to acquaint communities with it. And some went to the Provost's Office, and the idea caught on there. In January 1987 Mimi Orzech was authorized by the provost to set up a committee that would organize a week-long program—Holocaust Memorial Week—starting in April that year. And she built up the committee. She contacted—oh, I'd say about ten of us—I was one. I was the advisor to Hillel, the Jewish student group. But, more than that, I had been teaching a course on the Holocaust since 1982. . . . I very eagerly said, "Yes!" And I've been on the committee ever since. I doubt that any of us imagined that the committee or the program would still be around in 2023. But here we are, going strong.

Mimi remained chair until she retired from OSU in 1994, at which point I became the chair and have been ever since. . . . I still remember the first meeting that this committee had. Mimi introduced the various members. . . . . Then she talked a bit about her vision for the committee and for Holocaust remembrance. . . . [O]ne thing I can still hear her saying is that ours was going to be a "town and gown" exercise. This was not going to be just something to have on campus. We were going to have it in the public schools. Consequently, right away, members of the committee in that first go-around included a couple of teachers, and would later include administrators. We still have that: teachers and/or administrators being on the Holocaust committee. It's very important. We like having events in the schools. That was one principle. Another one was the breadth of the committee, including clergy right from the beginning, almost always Christian. [Holocaust Memorial Week and the committee] were going to involve the community. Likewise, we would have a representative from the government of the city of Corvallis. And so it went: integration, integration, integration right from the start.

As for the first few years of the Holocaust program, I've got to say—and this isn't at all surprising—that the first Holocaust Memorial Week observance in April 1987 was a very simple one. In fact, it was the simplest program we've ever had, of the thirty-six we've had. It consisted of one talk given by Sylvia Frankl, a fine scholar. She headed up the Oregon Holocaust Resource Center, which slightly predated [Holocaust Memorial Week at OSU]. She spoke about Christian rescuers of Jews during the Holocaust period. Beyond that, we showed a short documentary on the Holocaust. . . . We collected a lot of those posters that the Holocaust board had sent us from DC, and we had an exhibit. We had a display in the MU [Memorial Union at OSU]. And that was all there was to the initial Holocaust memorial week observance. Over the next few years, we kept expanding our offerings.

In 1989 we had our first Holocaust survivor named Fred Manela, who was then living in Eugene. . . . Fred had been active in a Jewish underground

Polish resistance hero and "witness to the Holocaust" Jan Karski (left), pictured here with Oregon State University President John Byrne (center) and Oregon Symphony Director James DePriest, pauses outside the Memorial Union before receiving an honorary doctorate from the university in 1990. During World War II, Karski secretly entered the Warsaw Ghetto and Izbica transit camp and endured torture to pass information to the Polish government-in-exile and bring evidence of the Nazis' genocidal assault on European Jews to the attention and consciences of Western Allies. In 1982, Yad Vashem honored Karski as "Righteous Among the Nations." Oregon State Photographic Collection. Courtesy of Oregon State University Special Collections and Archives Research Center, Corvallis, Oregon.

organization that warned Jews of the imminence of what came to be [known as] *Kristallnacht*, or the great violence against Jews in Germany in November 1938. Very interesting fellow. . . .

1990 was, I think, a year when our program was really launched. We had a second survivor named Murray Brown, also then living in Eugene. . . . [H]e had somehow survived seven camps, including four death camps, and talked at length about his experiences. But also that year we had Christopher Browning here. . . . His most famous work, *Ordinary Men*, was yet to be published, but he had completed the research for it and so he gave us, in essence, a preview. . . .

And another thing that we started to do that year was to video-record major events. Both Murray Brown's and Christopher Browning's talks were videoed. And they're part of that collection which now includes about sixty video events, most of which are available on YouTube.[1] So that tradition dates back to 1990. . . .

Up until 2000 or so, the Holocaust Memorial Week programs were heavily related to the Holocaust itself. However, after that, we started to broaden out, thinking in terms of comparative genocide. Because there is a concern that if—again I would say young people, and this includes university students, too—if all they're hearing about in the context of genocide is the Holocaust, [then] they can say, "Well, yeah, the Holocaust was a terrible thing, but that was a long time ago. And there hasn't been anything like that since or before. And so we don't have to worry about it too much."

So . . . in 2000, we decided to go in a somewhat different direction. Instead of having a very heavy emphasis on the Holocaust itself, or closely related topics, we decided to start having events on other genocides. . . . [O]ne thing that inspired this was that a member faculty at OSU wrote an op-ed on *The Barometer* [Oregon State's campus newspaper] in which she said that the Holocaust was a terrible thing, but there were other terrible things, too, that there were not enough observances related to at the university or elsewhere. She herself was Chinese and she talked about the atrocities in China during the Japanese occupation and especially the so-called "Rape of Nanking" in 1937. And it seemed to me that it would be really good to give over one night of Holocaust Memorial Week to a program—actually a film—and then a talk on the Japanese occupation. And so we did. And since then we have usually—many more years yes than no—had events on other genocides.

We had an extraordinary symposium in 2003 that was largely organized by Robert and Mary Jo Nye . . . on the persecution of gay men during the Holocaust. We, much more recently, had an excellent program on the genocide of the Roma. . . . We've had a couple excellent programs by very famous scholars on the Armenian genocide of the First World War. And we've had two programs on the Cambodian genocide. We've also expanded to cover wars, notably associated with atrocities. . . . We've broadened things out considerably, and I think that is really what we absolutely should be doing. So that people are more aware of the fact that obviously the Holocaust was a huge thing and a horrific thing. But it was not a unique event, aside from the ways in which any given wars or calamities can be unique. They all have their unique aspects.

You've had opportunities to talk to local survivors and survivors that have traveled to speak at Holocaust Memorial Week. How would you describe that experience and how has it impacted the way you taught the Holocaust here at OSU?

Well, I got some remarkable anecdotes from them and their talking about their experiences that I would tell my students in the Holocaust course. I brought them out considerably because these were people I'd spoken to extensively. But also [they were] just such remarkable people. . . . Holocaust survivors are truly a special breed. Obviously, they're quite elderly, the few who are left. And yet, as much as possible, they continue to come out and speak. And they especially like to speak to young audiences. The younger the better. I still remember one very noted Holocaust survivor. She was here in the mid 20-teens and I had arranged for her to speak at a synagogue up in Portland the day before she was due to speak down here [at OSU]. . . . [T]he audience that she had at the synagogue included people from a Jewish retirement home. Well, shall we say? It was a middle-aged audience typically. And I could tell, in fact, she made it clear that, you know: "Where were the kids?" She wanted to see kids [in the audience]. And I told her after the talk that, "It would be different once you spoke at OSU. There would be lots of young people there." And she looked at me rather dubiously.

But the next evening she came, and there was a huge turnout [at OSU]. [The audience] mostly, by considerable majority, were either OSU students or K-12 students. And at the end of her talk, she asked for questions, and . . . microphones were set up in the aisles. . . . [T]hose who lined up at the microphones were all young, [aged] twenty on down. And she was clearly pleased that they were there. And finally, I remember one boy coming to the mic to ask a question. And he was obviously pretty young, and he was speaking in a beautiful soprano voice. And she asked him how old he was. And he said thirteen. And you could just see her beam. That is what she wanted. That is what Holocaust survivors tend to want. They want young audiences.

For some years . . . starting in about 1992, one of the functions of the Holocaust Memorial Committee's teacher—or teachers—on the committee was to arrange for survivors to speak in the schools. There were some in the area who were Holocaust survivors. But the . . . Auschwitz survivors, general camp survivors, they were almost all in Portland. And so it was they'd have to drive down from Portland to come and speak in schools here. And I still remember—and this was maybe around 2004, 2005—two of my real favorites. I knew them both very well. Two women who were certainly into their eighties and were both Auschwitz survivors had come to speak in the schools. They'd driven down from Portland together, and I'd arranged for each of them to speak in two different schools that were fairly widely separated from each other. Anyway, I met up with them at Corvallis High School. They were looking a bit bedraggled. And I ask them how things went, and they said, "Oh, Paul this was just too hard to have to do two schools apiece." And I told them I would try to see if maybe we could start having just one school apiece in the future. And then I said, "But can I count on you for next year to come down here?" And they said, "Of course!" And they were so enthusiastic. They were instantly enthusiastic, "Yeah, yeah. Yeah!" The committee and I were going to set up the great opportunity for them to talk to young audiences. Talk about people who are driven. The Holocaust survivors who go out and speak are driven. It is just remarkable to see their dedication.

One of the reasons that the Holocaust Memorial Week really began was to combat antisemitism. How can educators combat antisemitism, Holocaust denial, and misinformation?

There is no doubt . . . antisemitism has just skyrocketed. And I must say that it began to rocket up in 2016 right after the election. . . . There's no real doubt that [antisemitism] is a problem. Now, what to do about the problem? . . . Maybe it's because I've been teaching for fifty years, but I am a great believer in the power of education. It is very encouraging that more and more states are mandating Holocaust education. For years there were eight [states that required Holocaust education] . . . and California was the only one west of the Mississippi. But now there has been a considerable upsurge. We have, I think, close to thirty at the moment that are mandating Holocaust education . . . and Oregon has become one of those. Now mind you, there were teachers who were teaching about the Holocaust long before this. It's now just that there's the mandate to do it. . . .

Holocaust education can do a lot. . . . And I think that, as important as it is to have teachers assigning *The Diary of a Young Girl* by Anne Frank, which they all do to their classes, that [students] should know something about the breadth of sources that one has on the Holocaust. . . . I think that the more teachers know about the Holocaust, that they should give their students a sense, whatever level they are, of why we know what we know. Where the information comes from.

You have spoken about how invaluable survivor speakers are to Holocaust education. How can we ensure that survivors' accounts are still impactful in the coming years when survivors are no longer with us?

Holocaust education is going to take a bad hit over the next ten, fifteen, twenty years as more and more of the remaining survivors pass on, or are too frail to continue to speak publicly. And that is going to hurt. The [OSU] Holocaust program experimented with inviting some very good speakers. They were not survivors, but the children of survivors. And they gave wonderful talks. . . . [The passing of survivors] is happening and that's unfortunate, but we need to be ready for it.

One thing that I would like to see is to not just show videos of survivors speaking, but to edit them and splice them so that they can be . . . answering particular questions about the Holocaust. "What was life like for you before 1939?" And carry them through. . . . There are several collections of survivor testimony. Some of these testimonies are more than eight hours long, very detailed. Others, perhaps thankfully, are much shorter than that. So why not combine them? Not just show them all full-blown, but combine them, make points with them, and then distribute them in the schools. That I think can be very helpful.

But we—those of us who are interested in Holocaust education—will have to be creative because the survivors themselves are not going to be around much longer.

Note

1 Many recordings from past Holocaust Memorial Week events can be accessed at https://holocaust.oregonstate.edu/videos.

Chapter Questions

CHAPTER 1: REFLECTIONS ON DISCRIMINATION, RACISM, AND STEREOTYPING

Essential Questions

- What role can individuals play in actively countering misinformation and discrimination directed at vulnerable groups?
- How do language and images that dehumanize vulnerable or marginalized groups influence and inspire legal restrictions and physical attacks on those groups?
- How might laws enacted by a government be utilized to inflict harm upon a population?

Reading Questions

- After the Nazis invaded the Netherlands, how did families like Laureen Nussbaum's adjust to the exclusion of Jews from recreational and cultural activities?
- According to Laureen Nussbaum, what was the experience of going to school like after labor deportations began in 1942?
- How did Marion Blumenthal Lazan's life and her family's life change after the Nazis took power?
- According to Marion Blumenthal Lazan, what was the Westerbork camp like when it was under the control of the Dutch government? How did the Westerbork camp change after the Nazis took control of it?
- What does Lucille Eichengreen's account of her father's tribulations reveal about the Nazi treatment of Polish Jews living in Germany?
- From whom did Lucille Eichengreen and her family receive abuse and antisemitic threats?

- Why did Eva Aigner's father move to Budapest? Why was he unable to obtain work locally?
- When did Eva Aigner first feel discriminated against?
- How does Jack Terry describe the attitudes of gentile Poles toward Jewish Poles?
- How does Stephen Nasser describe his treatment by non-Jewish people in Hungary?

Discussion Questions

- What was the purpose of Nazi laws that segregated Jews from non-Jewish populations and restricted Jewish economic opportunities?
- How did Marion Blumenthal Lazan and Lucille Eichengreen describe the November pogroms? Why were the November pogroms a turning point for many Jews?
- What does Walter Plywaski mean when he says, "This is the way mass murder starts. Not with a pistol shot, but by a titter and a smirk"?

CHAPTER 2: SEARCHING FOR REFUGE

Essential Questions

- What range of choices were available to European Jews seeking to escape perilous and life-threatening circumstances during the Nazi era?
- What factors influenced a person's likelihood of finding refuge from Nazi forces?
- What sorts of obstacles stood in the way of finding paths to safety?
- What specific choices or measures undertaken by individuals, communities, and governments can contribute to eliminating barriers and facilitating pathways to safety for those seeking refuge?

Reading Questions

- Why did Ursula Bacon's parents choose to go to China?
- What sorts of new responsibilities did Ursula Bacon take on when she and her family arrived in China?
- How did Ursula Bacon's family adjust to life and make ends meet while in Shanghai?

- What was Chella Velt Meekcoms Kryszek's time in hiding like?
- Why did Chella Velt Meekcoms Kryszek's family split up while hiding in the Netherlands?
- What does Chella Velt Meekcoms Kryszek's account reveal to us about the Dutch Underground?
- Why didn't Jacques Bergman's parents accompany him to the Netherlands? How did Jacques make his way while alone?
- According to Jacques Bergman, what was the original purpose of the Westerbork camp?
- What arrangements and preparations had Henry Friedman's father secretly made to keep his family out of the Brody ghetto and safe in hiding?
- What was Henry Friedman's experience like hiding as a fourteen-year-old? What difficulties and tragedies did he face?
- Why had the Semchuks momentarily considered poisoning Henry and his family?
- How did Toivi Blatt acquire false identification papers? Why did his attempt to get to Hungary fail?
- Who betrayed Toivi Blatt to the German forces? Why?
- What special responsibilities did Miriam Greenstein have as the only member of her family who could "pass" as a gentile?
- Why didn't Miriam Greenstein hide with her parents' gentile friends? What reason does she give?

Discussion Questions
- Why did countries like the United States do so little during the 1930s to aid refugees of Nazi persecution?
- To what extent did the experiences of Chella Velt Meekcoms Kryszek and Henry Friedman challenge your assumptions about what it would have been like to hide from the Nazis?

CHAPTER 3: RESISTANCE TO THE NAZIS

Essential Questions
- What sorts of factors influenced an individual's or a group's ability to engage in resistance?

- What forms of power can be exercised by people when they are deprived of control, authority, and safety?

Reading Questions

- What sort of labor did Toivi Blatt perform in Sobibor?
- When and why did Toivi Blatt and the prisoners at Sobibor decide they would revolt?
- How did the Sonderkommando at Auschwitz-Birkenau carry out their revolt?
- How did Ursula Bacon's life in China change after her family was forced into the Shanghai ghetto?
- How does Ursula Bacon describe school in the Shanghai ghetto?
- In what ways did ten-year-old Eva Mozes Kor defy the Nazis?
- How does Eva Mozes Kor describe her (and her sister Miriam's) experiences of Nazi medical experimentation?
- What advice did Itka Zygmuntowicz's parents impart to her after she was bullied and beaten by a group of Polish boys and girls before the German invasion?
- Why did Itka Zygmuntowicz whisper her name at roll call every morning?
- How did Stephen Nasser obtain a rare pencil in the Mühldorf labor camp?
- Why did Stephen Nasser go to so much trouble to keep a diary?
- How did Marion Blumenthal Lazan and her family cope with the dire conditions at Bergen-Belsen?
- What did Marion Blumenthal Lazan mean when she says that her games were her "survival techniques"?
- How did Ruth Kluger keep reading and learning while interned within Theriesenstadt, Auschwitz, and the Christianstadt labor camp?
- How did literature and poetry serve as "stabilizing life-savers" for Ruth Kluger?

Discussion Questions

- Why were the revolts at Sobibor and Auschwitz-Birkenau staged by prison laborers already there and not by new arrivals to the camp? What insight does Toivi Blatt provide?

- Why do you think it was important to Ursula Bacon's mother to have a tablecloth and a vase at the dining table while they were interned in the Shanghai ghetto?
- Given the difficult conditions of the Shanghai ghetto, why was it so important to establish an underground school?
- What do the recollections in Chapter 3 reveal about how forms and options of resistance differed in ghettos, labor camps, concentration camps, and killing centers?
- Which acts of resistance do you consider the most profound? Which acts of resistance surprised you?

CHAPTER 4: TAKING RISKS TO COMBAT INDIFFERENCE

Essential Questions
- How can acting with integrity make a difference even if you can't organize a movement?
- What motivates individuals to take risks in order to aid others?
- What moral responsibilities do individuals bear in addressing injustice, and how does standing up against injustice contribute to change?

Reading Questions
- According to George Wittenstein, how did the rise of the Nazi government impact life for non-Jewish Germans?
- What sorts of barriers to free and open communication did the Nazis create? What tactics did White Rose members use to communicate with each other and spread their messages?
- According to Knud Dyby, what was life like in Denmark under German occupation?
- What do you think made the Danish rescue effort so robust and successful? What challenges and dangers did members of the Danish resistance movement face?
- On what grounds (for what reasons) did Laureen Nussbaum's family receive their deferment for deportation?
- How does Laureen Nussbaum feel about non-Jewish citizens in the Netherlands and the Dutch resistance?

- What were the different initiatives that Eva Aigner's mother took to save her own life and the lives of her daughters?
- What sort of assistance did Alter Wiener receive at Gross Masselwitz?
- What does Jack Terry's speech reveal about the dynamics among prisoners in the Flossenbürg camp?
- What dangers did Jack Terry face in the Flossenbürg camp?
- Why did Walter Plywaski say that any Jewish person who ultimately survived the camps must have been "helped by someone who was not Jewish"?

Discussion Questions

- What motivated Knud Dyby and his co-conspirators in the Danish rescue movement?
- Why do you think fellow camp prisoners were willing to help Jack Terry and Walter Plywaski?
- Hans Calmeyer once remarked, "There are ridiculously small things that are possibly bigger than the great heroic deeds." Reflecting on the accounts in Chapter 4 (as well as Chapter 3), how did "small" actions and decisions make a significant, positive impact?

CHAPTER 5: TRANSITIONAL JUSTICE AND RECONCILIATION

Essential Questions

- In the aftermath of a mass atrocity, what strategies can individuals, communities, and governments employ to establish justice and foster peace?
- What measures can individuals, communities, and governments undertake to prevent the circumstances and patterns that precipitate persecution, conflict, and genocide?
- How might individuals, communities, and governments effectively respond to the needs of victims and survivors affected by mass atrocities?

Reading Questions

- Why did Les and Eva Aigner decide to start speaking publicly about their experiences during the Holocaust?

- What kinds of commemoration and reconciliation efforts have the Aigners participated in within Germany?
- What was the experience like for Les and Eva Aigner when they traveled back to Landsberg in 1995?
- What happened during Eva Mozes Kor's meeting with former Nazi doctor Hans Münch?
- Why, according to Eva Mozes Kor, is forgiveness such a powerful act?
- Why do you think it was important for Eva Mozes Kor to have Dr. Münch sign a statement about the use of gas chambers at Auschwitz?
- According to Thomas Buergenthal, what progress has been made since the Holocaust to affirm human rights and prevent genocide?
- In Thomas Buergenthal's opinion, what actions can people take right now to help promote human rights and prevent genocide?
- How would you compare Alter Wiener's and Jacques Bergman's views on forgiveness and justice after the Holocaust?
- Why did Jacques Bergman break his silence and begin to speak publicly about his experiences during the Holocaust?
- According to Marion Blumenthal Lazan, what efforts have the people of Hoya and the German government made to address Germany's horrific past and the crimes of the Holocaust?

Discussion Questions

- Several survivor speakers explained that, shortly after the war ended, no one wanted to hear about their experiences. Why do you think this was the case?
- Many speakers voiced their alarm about Holocaust denial. Have you ever witnessed Holocaust denial or Holocaust distortion (online or in person)?
- How can we counteract Holocaust denial and distortion in the twenty-first century?
- Why have incidents of antisemitism been rising since 2016 despite efforts to promote Holocaust education? What can individuals do to counteract antisemitism? What can institutions do? What can governments do?

Glossary of Key Terms

Antisemitism. According to the US Holocaust Memorial Museum, antisemitism means "prejudice against or hatred of Jews." Beyond animosity toward Jews, antisemitism involves a disregard for the individuality of Jewish personality or Jewish agency, and attributes negative and often threating qualities to *all* Jews.

Aryan. Term used by the Nazis to describe a supposed "race" of culturally and biologically superior light-skinned people from ancient India who migrated to Europe and became the forebears of European culture. The Nazis declared that non-Jewish Germans were descendants of this "Aryan race."

Asocial. Term the Nazis used to describe a variety of people that did not fit into the Nazi ideal for German society. The Nazis categorized the following people as "asocial": people with drug and alcohol problems, prostitutes, homeless people, the unemployed, homosexuals, and even members of Sinti and Roma communities. The Nazis frequently confined "asocials" to concentration camps.

Concentration Camp. Camps in which Nazi forces interned civilian populations deemed "disruptive" or "potentially dangerous." Conditions were brutal within camps; prisoners were subjected to hard labor and experienced poor living conditions and constant abuse from guards and even fellow prisoners. Although many prisoners died or were murdered at these camps, they are distinct from killing centers (see definition). The first Nazi-run concentration camps were opened in 1933 within Germany but continued to function and evolve throughout WWII.

Death March. Forced evacuations of Nazi-run camps and killing centers in German-occupied territories carried out in the winter of

1944–1945 to avoid encroaching Russian forces during the final months of the war. Camp prisoners were forced to travel tens to hundreds of miles by foot or open rail car to rail stations and other German camps located further west. Thousands of prisoners were shot by SS guards for walking slowly; many others died of exhaustion, hypothermia, and starvation.

Gentile. Noun and adjective to describe a person who is not Jewish.

Gestapo. Nazi Germany's secret state police force.

Ghetto. Term that generally refers to a particular and confined region of a city or town in which a minoritized group is required to inhabit. During WWII, Nazi forces established ghettos as "holding-places" for Jews in German-occupied territories. German forces often extracted wealth and labor from Jews interned within ghettos. Ghettos were notoriously overcrowded and under-resourced; hundreds of thousands of Jews died within Nazi-run ghettos due to disease, hunger, and brutality.

Holocaust Denial. According to the USHMM, "Holocaust denial is any attempt to negate the established facts of the Nazi genocide of European Jews." Historian Deborah Lipstadt has further categorized Holocaust denial into two camps of "hard-core" and "soft-core" denial. Hard-core Holocaust denial takes the form of claiming that no systematic murder of European Jews by Nazi forces occurred. Soft-core Holocaust denial usually acknowledges some Jewish deaths but maintains that the total number of Jewish deaths was significantly lower (often by orders of several million) than the historical consensus of around 6 million deaths. Holocaust deniers often specialize in attacking the credibility of survivor testimony.

Holocaust Distortion. Holocaust distortion encompasses a broad set of beliefs and actions that misrepresent the Holocaust or minimize the history of the Holocaust for political or ideological purposes. Most commonly, Holocaust distortion does not question whether the Holocaust happened. Holocaust distortion may be motivated by antisemitism. Some additional motivations for Holocaust distortion can include ignorance of the actual extent of Jewish persecution and suffering during the Holocaust or the desire of governments to avoid acknowledging and contending with atrocities committed by their nationals during WWII.

Kapo. Concentration camp and labor camp prisoners granted special authority by the SS to discipline and supervise fellow prisoners.

Killing Centers. Nazi-run centers constructed in occupied Poland for the purpose of executing large numbers of people considered to be political and racial enemies of the Reich. Between December 1941 and the end of the war, nearly 2.7 million Jews were murdered in killing centers built at Chelmno, Belzec, Treblinka, Sobibor, and Auschwitz-Birkenau (or Auschwitz II). These killing centers were often located near concentration or labor camps, but killing centers shared little in common with concentration camps. Prisoners were not "concentrated" or merely detained at killing centers; they were murdered immediately, or spared briefly in order to be forced to assist with the murder of new arrivals (see Sonderkommando).

Kindertransport. Name given to a series of rescue efforts launched by private citizens and Jewish aid organizations to bring Jewish children from Nazi Germany (and Nazi-occupied Austria and parts of Czecho-slovakia) to safety in England and the Netherlands between 1938 and 1940.

Kristallnacht. See *November pogroms*.

November pogroms. Series of orchestrated attacks against Jewish communities, synagogues, individuals, and Jewish homes and businesses carried out across the German Empire on November 9–10, 1938. The Nazis referred to the events as *Kristallnacht*, or "Crystal Night," or "The Night of Broken Glass," due to the tremendous amount of glass shattered during attacks on Jewish homes, businesses, and synagogues. Perpetrators of the attack, led by members of the *Sturmabteilung* (Stormtroopers, or SA) and the Hitler Youth, killed at least 100 Jews during the pogroms. In addition, around 30,000 Jewish men were systematically apprehended and sent to German concentration camps.

Nuremberg Laws. Series of Nazi laws promulgated in September 1935 that legally categorized Jews as biological and political outsiders. The

"Law for Protection of German Blood and Honor" prohibited marriage and sexual relations between Jews and so-called "Aryan" Germans. The second, "Reich Citizenship Law," stripped away most civil and political rights from Jews by defining them as mere "subjects," no longer citizens, of the German Empire.

Pogrom. The term "pogrom" originated in late-nineteenth-century Russia to describe the violent attacks and massacres perpetrated against Jews in Eastern Europe at that time. The word means "riot" or "destruction" in Russian. In its contemporary usage, a "pogrom" is an organized attack on the lives and property of a marginalized group in order to eliminate the group or terrorize the group into leaving a particular area.

Sonderkommando. German term meaning "special unit." In Nazi-run killing centers, Sonderkommandos were prisoners whose lives were spared temporarily while the SS forced them to assist with the killing processes. Typically, members of the Sonderkommando collected and sorted belongings of the dead and carried out the cremation processes after executions.

SS. Abbreviated form of "Schutzstaffel" (German for "protection squads), the SS was first established in 1929 to serve as bodyguards for Hitler and high-ranking Nazis and grew in power under Heinrich Himmler's leadership. The SS collected information on political opponents, controlled the German police, and maintained "security" in the German empire before and during WWII. SS agents managed concentration camps and were chiefly responsible for organizing and implementing acts of genocide.

Synagogue. A place of Jewish worship that also serves as a site of religious learning and community activities.

Wehrmacht. The united armed forces of Germany.

Index

Italic type indicates an image.